Successfully Buy Your Franchise:

Expert Advice from a Business Broker

I0473762

By Andrew Rogerson

Certified Business Intermediary (CBI)
Certified Business Broker (CBB)
Certified Machinery and Equipment Appraiser (CMEA)
Certified Senior Business Analyst (CSBA)

www.Andrew-Rogerson.com

Published by
RBS
Rogerson Business Services
Sacramento, CA
www.businesstransactionbooks.com

Rogerson Business Services
777 Campus Commons Road, Suite 200
Sacramento, CA, 95825
www.businesstransactionbooks.com

Successfully Buy Your Franchise: Expert Advice from a Business Broker
Copyright © 2008-2009 Andrew Rogerson, CBI, CBB, CMEA, CSBA

ISBN: 978-1-4775456-1-4

Library of Congress Registration Number: TX-7-071-315

Disclaimer

This publication is designed to provide accurate and helpful information about buying a franchise. It is sold with the understanding that the author is NOT engaged in offering legal, accounting, or any other professional advice. Please consult a competent professional for assistance.

Acknowledgements

Business Brokerage Press
International Franchise Association (IFA)
The Business Reference Guide by Tom West
International Business Brokers Association (IBBA)
California Association of Business Brokers (CABB)
International Franchise Association (IFA) Franchise University
The Resource Handbook for Business Brokers and Intermediaries by Tom West
Ultimate Guide to Personal Finance for Entrepreneurs by Peter Sander with J Jeff Lambert

Special Thanks

Special thanks to the following for contributing to the text and/or checking the details: Anne Rogerson, Roger Murphy, Tim Rogers, Greg Roquet, Stephanie Chandler, Jerry Tsai, Tom Miller, Diane Miller, and Fred Hall.

Special Acknowledgment Of IBBA

The International Business Brokers Association is a global organization that advances the professional development of over 1,800 member intermediaries, educates potential clients about the value of intermediary services, and promotes the highest possible standards of ethical conduct. IBBA sponsors national education programs and conferences twice each year and cooperates with state and local business broker's organizations to conduct "grass roots" programs for the benefit of business communities around the country. IBBA awards the prestigious designation of Certified Business Intermediary (CBI) to members who demonstrate professional excellence through their Iintermediary experience and education and pass a comprehensive examination. Andrew Rogerson holds the CBI designation.

For more information contact:

International Business Brokers Association
401 North Michigan Avenue, 24th Floor
Chicago, IL 60611-4267
Phone: 888-686-4222   Fax: 312-673-6599
E-mail: admin@ibba.org
Web: www.ibba.org

Special Acknowledgment Of CABB

The California Association of Business Brokers is a professional trade association whose members are actively involved in assisting their clients in buying, selling, and evaluating businesses. CABB was organized to recognize the professionals of business opportunity brokerage, to help educate the public on the benefits of using licensed intermediaries, and to establish a code of ethics to which members adhere. CABB awards the prestigious designation of Certified Business Broker (CBB) to members who demonstrate professional excellence through their intermediary and business brokerage experience and education and pass a series of examinations. Andrew Rogerson holds the CBB designation.

For more information contact:

California Association of Business Brokers
1215 K Street, Suite 2290
Sacramento, CA, 95814
Phone: 866-972-2220   Fax: 916-231-2141
E-mail: cabb@cabb.org
Web: www.cabb.org

Table Of Contents

Section Four: Let's Get Started

Section Five: Validations

Section Six: Review Your Options

Section Seven: Final Steps

Section Eight: Additional Information

Welcome!

When an entrepreneur first decides to look at business ownership, it generally sets off a series of complex and confusing questions as well as an emotional roller coaster. The complex and confusing questions include; will I buy an existing business or start my own? If I start my own business, what will I do and will it be successful? How do I know if it will be successful? There are several options including starting and buying an existing business. However, if business ownership is the direction you would like to take, you have a third option and that is buying the rights to a franchise.

Although the road to business ownership has three different paths, this workbook is built for one purpose only and that is to help a business owner who is considering the option to buy the rights to a franchise and open a business from scratch with the help of their franchisor. A separate workbook is available on buying an existing business which will be more helpful to those who decide to start a new business from scratch. Please look for my workbook called Successfully Start Your Own Business: Expert Advice from a Business Broker.

If this workbook has one purpose, it has two goals. The first goal is to outline and inform the reader about the different tasks and questions a franchise buyer will have to decide as they move through the decision-making process. The second goal is to provide a means for the franchise buyer to plan, organize, and prepare so when they buy their franchise they are better organized and understand what's happening at each point in the transaction. The third goal is about helping you understand what's involved in buying the rights to a franchise, determine what's important to you, and work through your options so you can ultimately arrive at the decision that makes sense for you. Notice I said "arriving at the decision that makes sense for *you*." Not your spouse. Not your parents, family, best friend, neighbor, accountant, mentor, coach, consultant, or advisor…but *YOU*. This is your life and your decision.

The inspiration for this guide comes from my personal experiences in buying, selling, owning, and operating five businesses in two countries, researching many, many different types of businesses, and my current experience as a business consultant/broker to those that wish to exit or enter business ownership. I wish someone had given me some organized structure to tackle this difficult experience as I have had to learn it the hard way. Now my goal is to use my experiences to help make that journey easier for you.

There are so many nuances to starting or buying a business, whether it is a franchise or not. Each person's experience is unique as it brings together not only the different experiences of that person and those of their families, but also the attorneys, accountants, landlords, finance companies, franchisors, and other professionals that may assist in the transaction.

Please use this workbook to make notes along the way. This is a guide to read, learn, and stimulate thoughts. Please write down thoughts you have and check them out later so you don't lose track of them and are ultimately better prepared. If you prefer to scribble notes before finalizing your thoughts, photocopy the pages so you can have one final version to work through as you arrive at different decision points in the transaction.

Just so I am clear, if you fill in the pages in the guide exactly as its written you are a very lucky person. You should expect to talk with different people with different life and business experiences. If you expect the transaction to flow EXACTLY as it is outlined in this guide, then you will be disappointed. However, if you follow the steps as closely as possible, you will have a much greater chance of success. So be patient as you travel your journey of buying your franchise.

Your Goals And Tasks

Use the chart below to write down major goals or tasks that come to mind that you feel you must do to successfully buy your franchise. Refer back to this chart as you read through this guide so that you can add and remove items you want to complete and stay up-to-date.

Goal/Task Description	Start Date	Completion Date

Idea Tracker

As you read this guide, it will inspire ideas or prompt action items. Use the space below to jot down and track these ideas so you can organize your thoughts into action items.

Idea	Action needed	Completed

Your Feedback

The goal of this guide is to help small business owners through the process of buying their franchise in the quickest time possible but before making that final decision, feel they have left no rock unturned and answered every question on their mind. Although all business buyers have the same objective—to buy their business—the journey to achieving that goal is never the same.

There are a wide variety of factors that affect the entire process:

- ✓ Each buyer has unique personal differences be it the type of industry they choose, whether they want a service or product driven business, or the amount of money available to buy a business, etc.
- ✓ The business background the buyer comes from.
- ✓ The professional support services the buyer chooses to consult or hire.
- ✓ The current direction of the economy.
- ✓ The current state of the industry the buyer chooses to enter.
- ✓ If finance is required, there are many difference sources, be it family and friends or institutions such as banks or credit unions.
- ✓ Taxes and related laws that often change.

Because of these factors and many others, I strongly advise you to seek the assistance of experts at different stages of your purchase. We'll cover these as we work through the different phases but help from a person with financial experience is always a great idea as well as help from an attorney experienced with franchises.

If you have comments or suggestions that you feel would improve this guide and you have a moment to share, please e-mail your suggestions to info@Andrew-Rogerson.com.

With thanks,

Andrew Rogerson

The Golden Rule

There is no such thing as a stupid question.

General Information

> *"The future belongs to people that see possibilities before they become obvious."*
>
> *Ted Levitt*

Introduction

The steps to buying a franchise are numerous, sometimes complex, and at times, very frustrating. The major purpose of this guide is to outline and explain the many steps to buying a franchise, why they need to be taken, and when to take them if you decide to buy a franchise. With this information, this guide can reduce the number of steps or missteps that you may take, thereby reducing the costs, time spent, complexity, and frustration. Owning and operating a franchise is not for everyone. But hopefully by following these steps, it will allow you to make that determination on your own, as there are great personal, financial, and emotional rewards in business ownership.

This guide is written from a different perspective. It is not written from the perspective of a franchisor, accountant, attorney, financial planner but that of a business broker. My current profession is that of a business broker. I help business owners exit business ownership or buyers enter business ownership. I get into the nitty gritty of a business and see what's happening, what's done well, what could be done better and how both sides in the transaction always seeing things differently but with my job to bring everyone together. It is this perspective I bring to this guide. The questions I ask, the process I use, and the dynamic I bring also comes from my business brokering experience as well as owning 5 businesses.

And remember, this guide is built to be used. Make notes and use the templates to jot down ideas as they come to mind so you can refer back to them. The buying of your franchise is unique and you can customize this guise to suit your situation. One of the main reasons for publishing this in workbook format is so that you can write in it, customize, and use the information to be successful in buying your franchise in the quickest time possible.

The flow of the guide is as follows:
✓ Section one provides general information on some of the concepts and terms you may come across when buying your franchise.
✓ Section two introduces a brief history of franchising, the different formats of franchising, the benefits of franchising, and other general information about franchising including the documents you will use.
✓ Section three covers planning so you can build strong foundations to see if buying a franchise is your best business ownership option as well as incorporate some of the topics covered earlier.
✓ Sections four through six cover the actual process of buying a franchise so you can get to section seven and make a final decision.
✓ Section eight has some additional information that hopefully you will find useful, while the last section includes a glossary of terms so that you can better understand the industry terminology.

Please write down any terms you come across that aren't familiar to you. If they aren't covered in the glossary, you are welcome to e-mail them to me at info@Andrew-Rogerson.com and I will add them to the next edition of the guide. You are also welcome to e-mail questions about buying your franchise.

Tip: Write down your Questions

Never leave a question you ask unanswered –
It's your responsibility to be fully informed before you make the final decision.

Business Ownership – What Are My Options?

So you've decided to consider business ownership, but are not sure where to start?

Basically there are only three options: first, start a business from scratch with your own idea, second, buy an existing business or third, try a combination of one and two and buy the rights to a franchise to open it from scratch.

Below is a table that captures each of the three options and then attempts to lay out the different risks or variables associated with each idea. I've included this table to give you some talking or thinking points to see if you can find one option that makes more sense to you than the others. The list below is not exhaustive so please use the table on the next page to add other ideas that are important to you. Doing so may create action items for you to research further so write them down as well. If you have questions, challenges, suggestions or simply want to vent, please email me at info@andrew-rogerson.com

	Start new business	*Buy existing business*	*Buy a franchise*
Availability	None	Limited	Many
Established business methodologies	None	Hopefully	Yes
Documented processes	None	Limited - if at all	Yes
Training	None	Initial 2 weeks or so	Initial and ongoing
Investment V Profit	None	Yes	None
Support during ownership	None	None	Yes
Risk	Highest	Unknown until you're the owner	Many variables
Finance availability	Very difficult	Yes	Yes
How to predict success	Success based on projections	Success comes from history only	Success based on feedback from current owners
Decision maker	Owner	Owner	Follow the system
Instant cash flow	No	Yes	No
Established customer relationships	No	Yes	No
Established relationship with suppliers	No	Yes	Maybe
Established reputation	No	Yes	Yes
Established brand	No	Yes	Yes

Use the table below to write down additional ideas you consider important to include when deciding which business option to pursue.

Idea	Start new business	Buy existing business	Buy a franchise

Write down any ideas you want to research further.

How Do I Know If Business Ownership Is Right For Me?

This is possibly a burning question as you consider different options, especially if what you are currently doing is not rewarding and want to do something else. What are your options? Do you find a new job, stay in your current position, or move into business ownership? As you look for answers to this question I suggest there may be many suggestions from those around you. Ultimately, the final answer will come from you and you alone. Deciding if business ownership is right for you includes many emotions and motivations. These may include:

- ✓ No more layoffs
- ✓ Having control of your work and personal life
- ✓ Having balance with work, family, and friends
- ✓ Financial security
- ✓ Personal fulfillment
- ✓ Success
- ✓ Creating and building something
- ✓ Contributing to the community
- ✓ Family involvement
- ✓ No company politics
- ✓ Less frustration and job stress
- ✓ Getting away from the corporate life

Perhaps I forgot the most important motivation – money. I think a major reason most people enter business ownership is because they believe they can make more money than what they currently earn and perhaps what they will earn in the foreseeable future. What's interesting is that according to the book, the Millionaire Next Door, five out of six millionaires earn their fortunes through business ownership.

How else do I decide?

Part of the purpose of this guide is to take you through the decision-making process so you can decide if buying a franchise makes sense to you. We'll explain shortly how I use a consultative process to go through franchise ownership options to help you understand the buying process, determine what's important to you, and work through your options so you arrive at the decision that makes sense for you. Notice I said "arriving at the decision that makes sense for you." That's the purpose of this guide or workbook and that is, allowing you to arrive at the decision that makes sense to you. Not your spouse. Not your parents, family, best friend, neighbor, accountant, mentor, coach, consultant, or advisor…but YOU.

Here are some other things to consider.

Goals

I think you would agree that all successful people have goals. I suspect that even unsuccessful people have goals, but they perhaps lack the discipline, organizational skills, personal drive, education, and chutzpah, or perhaps they are unlucky. Maybe they are on the path to success but just haven't got there yet. Either way, if you've decided business ownership is something you want to consider, I expect the underlying drive is that you have goals and you see business ownership as the means to get there. In many cases, one of the underlying goals you have is personal wealth.

Entrepreneur V Intrapreneur

On page 14 we mentioned the 3 ways of entering business ownership – start from scratch, buy an existing business, or start a franchise. (Yes, can you can buy an existing franchise but that's covered by option two.)

Perhaps the way to work out the best option for you is by a process of elimination. The key ingredients I would suggest to successfully **start a new business** includes:

1. A business idea not currently in the market or an improvement on an existing idea. The key is that the market will pay you enough to make it worth your while in terms of both money and time invested to get a return on your investment.
2. The money to fund your business idea plus keep you fed, clothed, and housed until you turn it into a commercial success.
3. The complete business skills package to develop the idea and perfect it, and then build and deploy the sales and marketing, operation, management, and financial systems to turn a profit.
4. The personality, education, personal skills, and drive to see this through to a profit.

(If this is how you see yourself, read no further as this guide is not for you. What may help you is another of my workbooks called "Successfully Start Your business: Expert Advice from a Business Broker."

If you are deciding on whether to buy an existing business or **buy a franchise and start from scratch**, consider the following: Are you an Entrepreneur or an Intrapreneur?

My perception is that most main street business owners are either an entrepreneur or an intrapreneur. I see the entrepreneurs as those that prefer running their own privately held company and with the following characteristics:

- ✓ Highly independent
- ✓ Visionary
- ✓ Comfortable accepting higher risks
- ✓ Somewhat of a loner

I see Intrapreneurs as those that prefer owning and operating a franchise, and they tend to have the following characteristics:

- ✓ Tend to be more conservative
- ✓ Open to expert guidance
- ✓ Often more methodical, tending to mitigate risks
- ✓ Likes interaction with franchisor and other franchisees
- ✓ Worked in Corporate America, possibly in a management role and so understands reporting structures, accountability, project timelines and working to achieve deadlines

But how do I know if business ownership is right for me?

From the research I've done and from my personal experience, I honestly don't think there is a black and white answer. I think the hardest part of pursuing business ownership is making that initial decision. My decision to move into business ownership came from the lack of alternatives. I looked at the bosses I'd worked for and the people I knew in small business and concluded that I could do all and sometimes more than the bosses I reported to. I also looked at people I knew in business ownership and decided I could match what they did if I paid attention to detail, sought opinions from those that were successful and believed in myself. A couple of other thoughts:

A critical ingredient of successful business owners that I have been able to observe is a personality trait of being a positive thinker. Running and owning a business is not easy; especially if there are self doubts. Having a positive attitude that looks through those difficult times is a very important attribute.

The other critical things I did were understand that business ownership came with risks. My success would be increased if I managed the risk of running a business by paying everyone when they were due, making sure the customer's expectations were exceeded and paying attention to detail. All this sounds a bit simplistic but I've found it successful with the five businesses that I've owned. And perhaps another critical ingredient is having the support of those immediately around you such as your spouse and immediate family. Because they know who you are and understand you the best, they can support you when there are challenges running a business; and I am yet to talk to a business owner that hasn't experienced challenges. As they say, if it was easy, everyone would do it.

So how do you really know if business ownership is right for me? You don't. In the Aboriginal community of Australia they have a saying, No Dream, No Story, No Song. Dreaming is a critical part of Aboriginal life in Australia. The significance of dreaming is that it's used to inspire positive emotions to take action. The Aboriginal communities love telling stories. Because of their isolated environment and the fact they are nomadic, books were not part of their culture. However their culture is critical to them both individually and collectively. The way to educate their children and pass on their culture is through stories. Stories about drought, flood or hunting etc. Finally, the other way of passing things on and remembering things is through song. Like a book, a song would be used to explain an historic event or even to give directions. Water is critical in the remote parts of Australia. If you don't have a book or a map, how do you give directions to food or water? You do it through a song that explains how to get from point A to point B and how long it all takes.

So the point of the above is that either you believe in yourself and believe in your dream of business ownership and go for it or no dream, no story and no song.

Perhaps you would welcome talking to a SCORE counselor? SCORE is a non- profit organization that provides counseling services for potential or existing small business owners. They have local chapters throughout the United States where you can make an appointment with a counselor and get their free advice on business ownership including operating, marketing, financial advice etc. They have a website at http://www.score.org where you can go to get more information and also easily navigate to their local chapter and phone or email to make an appointment to visit one of their counselors or advisors.

How Do I Decide Which Franchise Is Right For Me?

At the time of writing this guide I have about 120 franchises for sale a buyer can choose from. Almost without exception, most buyers want to buy a franchise where they live. Some buyers wish to relocate but that is the exception rather than the rule. Because franchises are being continuously bought there is a constant change of inventory and so each buyer I work with is unique. Each time the process we use is different but always involves consultations, research, investigation, reflection and decisions/action.

Overview of the buying process

A common early question I get is "what's the process and how long will it take?" The second part of the question is easier to answer. It will take as long as you want it to take and as long as it takes till you can reach your decision. That's a bit of a smart answer but there is truth in it as the final "yes" or "no" decision can't be made until you have all the facts, fully digested all the variables and feel emotionally ready to make a decision. As a "rule of thumb" I like to suggest it takes between 6 to 8 weeks to work through the process, when working about 8 hours per week on it.

In simple terms there are 13 steps to buying your franchise. These are:
1. Research business ownership so you understand what's involved and decide if this is something you definitely want to do or find out more about. If it is, start making a business plan.
2. First meeting with your consultant. Bring your business plan if you're ready to share.
3. Completion of the questionnaire.
4. Second meeting with your consultant to go over the questionnaire and arrive at 2 or 3 franchises for you to research.
5. Receive, read and review the Franchise Disclosure Document.
6. Research questions/material from the franchisor and update your business plan. Make validation calls, do more research and continue to refresh your business plan.
7. Continue to work with the team you have assembled including the advisors, consultant and franchisor contact. If everything is making sense, schedule a Discovery Day with the franchisor.
8. Attend the Discovery Day. More research, if necessary. Refresh your Business Plan.
9. Secure finance.
10. Sign the Franchise Agreement.
11. Attend corporate training.
12. Attend Local training.
13. ...so you can open for business.

Franchising Is Not For Everyone.

There is no question that franchising is not for everyone. In fact, business ownership, be it starting a new business from scratch or buying an existing business, is not right for everyone. To help you decide if franchising is right for you, consider the following.

1. Franchisees are independent business people. By definition, a franchise has an operating system that the franchisee needs to follow as it's this operating system that has made the franchise successful. If the franchisee is too independent (or a true entrepreneur) then this would not be a good fit.
2. Owning any business requires hard work, often long hours and always an element of risk and a franchise is no different. With the opportunity of great success also comes the risk of failure. If you are not comfortable with these ideas, then franchising would not be a good fit.
3. Some critics suggest that franchisees can be taken advantage of by the franchisor or that the frequency of litigation is high. The answer to this is that the Franchise Disclosure Document (FDD) reports that information so you can see firsthand for yourself what is happening. Just as it's important to see the turnover of franchisees leaving the system, the FDD also provides the contact details of the current franchisees so you can give them a call and get their feedback. This is a huge benefit. How many business owners can you call when you start a new business to find out how they are doing? How many business owners can you call that are operating a similar business to one you may plan on buying and will take the time to explain their successes and failures?
4. The franchisor controls the process with requirements such as the minimum hours of operation, the minimum number of employees on the premises at the same time, the amount of inventory or the maximum prices are charged. Once again, this may be true but this is the advantage of the system a franchisor brings. They have done research and experience to support their conclusions. The FDD will once again make those disclosures so it's clear to you those requirements and you can decide before you buy your franchise.
5. Franchisors are built to sell franchises to "Mom and Pop" buyers who aren't sure what they are doing. Perhaps you know someone that bought a franchise and it wasn't successful and this was their experience. One experience does not make for a "truth." Similarly, there's absolutely no upside to a franchisee failing – everyone loses. For this reason and it tends to be overlooked, when a buyer is weighing up whether or not to buy a franchise it goes both ways – the franchisor is also weighing up whether the buyer would fit be a fit with them.

If you have questions or concerns about buying a franchise, my suggestion is to keep an open mind, but do the research to see if your concerns are valid. It is true that franchising is not for everyone. It's equally true that business ownership is not for everyone. But it's even truer – only you should get to make that final decision and I would suggest, only after doing the research and weighing all the options.

No Dream, No Story, No Song - 8 Dream Killers.

As we just mentioned, franchising is not for everyone. Equally, business ownership is not for everyone. My main goal in writing this guide is to provide as much information as possible in as logical order as possible so you can make that final decision yourself. I'm sure you have heard it before that someone observed that everyone is an expert in at least two areas: raising *your* kids and leading *your* life. My children tell me that all the time. Perhaps there should be a third: running *your* business or more succinctly, owning *your* business. Everyone loves to think they are helping - it's only human nature. We all have our opinions and we love nothing more than sharing them – be they valuable or not. And because they are delivered with such good intention, when the advice isn't followed we are made to feel bad. Perhaps the hardest advice we get or hear are the "horror" stories from people who are close to us. Bottom line – it's your life; you get to make the final decision – and that's the way it should be.

So here are eight reasons you can use not to buy your franchise. Incidentally, I have explained why the eight reasons are not valid but in the end you get to make that final decision – that's what following your dream is all about.

1. A 'loved one' or spouse dream killer: This is probably the most important of them all. The business buyer talks it over with his loved one or significant other and thinks they have agreement they will buy a business or franchise. When the decision day comes the agreement is not as forthcoming as first thought as objections and concerns begin to flow.

Answer: Owning a business, be it a franchise or any business must be arrived at as a *joint decision*. Business ownership will impact your family in a way that a having a job change doesn't. If it's scary for you, imagine how it must feel to those around you. They have less information about what you are thinking of doing or they may not be as informed. Even before the search begins, a married couple needs frank, honest discussions about the benefits and problems of business ownership. When there is agreement to go forward, both parties should attend any discussions so each has the same information. The added benefit of doing this is that each will remember different information so if one has unanswered questions and the other does not have the answer, it will require getting the answer so you can move forward.

2. The "Passion" dream killer: Often you will hear or read that you must have a "passion" for your product or service. And if you don't have that passion, don't get involved. How much passion can you maintain changing the oil or doing a lube at an AAMCO or MAACO business or removing a computer virus from your Tech Hero franchise?

Answer: There are two important points. Firstly, you are running a business and it's your responsibility as the owner to run it correctly by following the appropriate laws, ensuring customer service is as high as possible, all the bills are paid etc. If you don't run the business properly then everything goes away. Secondly, the "passion" you need is building a viable and ongoing business so you can feed and maintain you and/or your family and then make some money when you sell your business. *Passion for building a business is also a great passion to have* and it well may be that the product or service is just incidental in that case.

3. The friend or neighbor dream killer: Not only does everyone love to be asked for their advice but even more they love to give it. When you buy a new car or get a job promotion or have big news we love to share it with friends and neighbors; that's why they are family and friends. Unfortunately

telling others what we do seems to automatically provide the right to give their advice even if they do not know anything about the subject. I'm always ready to give my opinion on anything! Just ask!

Answer: Without being rude or close minded, try to limit the input from well meaning, but non-expert people. Some buyers I've worked with have said that they never discuss their plans with family or friends simply because they do not want to be burdened with the uninformed opinions of others.

4. The "Been there – done that" dream killer: This one's real simple. You are bound to know family, friends or work colleagues that considered business ownership and for whatever reason they decided not to move forward with it. So when they hear of your plans to buy a franchise they like nothing more than explaining in great detail why you shouldn't. It's not pleasant to contemplate, but sometimes your decision to explore new horizons may create envy, resentment, or fear, from people you know. It sounds silly. Why should someone else resent the step you are about to make? Sad to say, envy and jealousy are common human failings, and may exist even in your circle of friends and acquaintances. So, if you are taking a giant step forward, your "friend" may feel he/she is being left behind! Rather than join you on the journey to new successes, however, the "envious associate" will find good *sounding* reasons to justify doing nothing. By stopping you from moving forward, your associate justifies his inability to move.

Answer: Focus on YOUR goals, and tune out uninformed or ill reasoned advice, whatever the source. It does not matter whether the person who is trying to hold you back is doing it for the right reasons or not. All that matters is if the advice is accurate and solid. If it is, then pay attention to it.

5. The "cold feet" dream killer: Probably the most common dream killer, and unfortunately it is self inflicted. Yep - we do it to ourselves. Buying or going into business is probably one of the three biggest decisions we make in life next to choosing a spouse and buying your first house. If you have a spouse or have at least bought one home you can remember the thought you gave and how it was a little bit scary. Deciding to go into business is a big thing, and it is definitely scary. So what can happen is that we set up a way to avoid that hard and scary decision by finding reasons to justify *not* going into business. We allow our fears to get ahead of our hopes. We deprive ourselves of the opportunity to achieve the very thing we most want...the independence, security and freedom that comes with being the boss of a successful business.

Answer: We must embrace being scared and use the fear factor to our advantage by letting it add an extra element of caution and care to our research. After you have clearly set your goals through your business plan, you must compare several different opportunities to each other to see which one most closely matches your "perfect model business."

6. The "sample of one" dream killer: Too often buyers will get a feedback from one person about a particular business and make all future decisions on that one piece of feedback. Advice from just one person is always dangerous, and unfortunately this one works in both directions. For example, you may talk with someone who failed in that business or worse yet, just in the particular industry. As a result the buyer concludes the business is not for them - a rash conclusion. And conversely, the buyer hears one single success story and decides this is the business for them. Another rash conclusion!

Answer: A "sample of one" is always dangerous as it is too limited. Also, it should not be attempted until one has a solid core of data collected over time from many reliable sources. Bottom line; check multiple opinions from multiple sources and take care to ask the same questions the same way so you get a complete picture. Don't ask multiple people a different set of questions as you have no true basis for comparison of whether your final decision is positive or negative about the business, and whether it is a good "fit."

7. The "wrong set of questions" dream killer: Often buyers destroy their own dreams of business ownership by confusing casual inquiry with real research. For example, a buyer considering a retail business may try to find how many similar businesses are listed in the Yellow Pages. That's an interesting idea or data point but it doesn't indicate the real size of that market, if it's a niche market, the proximity of each business to each other etc. It may well be that market in that area is under-served!

Similarly, a buyer may ask a *competitor* about the business opportunity. Do you expect a competitor to encourage you to enter their field? None of this "looking around" is valid research. It falls into the "interesting, but so what" category.

Another example: a person has a valid concern about a business. Perhaps they heard that staffing is a challenge. Or maybe there are fears the market is already crowded with competitors. These questions should be researched with the true experts in the business: the franchisor and the franchisees – otherwise your dream may be lost.

Answer: You must do your own research about the industry and the franchise. **The best source of information about the franchise is the franchisor and the franchisees.** This is because they have already conducted their research and built their business plan accordingly. Ask for a copy of their business plan but you must get a copy of the Franchise Disclosure Document (FDD), which only the franchisor can supply. Not only does the FDD provide a good deal of information about the business opportunity, it also supplies the list of current franchisees. You need to speak to as many of them as you can to get more data about the franchise. Also, information about the industry size, stability, and growth may be available from business journals and books available at local and college libraries. Ask the librarian for assistance.

8. Paralysis by analysis: Another form of dream killer, this describes people who never make a decision because their research never ends. Intense personal due diligence on any business opportunity is a must. We strongly advocate doing everything from talking to business owners in like businesses and/or franchises, to consulting professional advisors. Also, seek out *qualified* advice; but make sure it's qualified. Of course, talk to others in the same type of business that you are contemplating. Seek out attorneys, CPA's, and other qualified business experts but stay away from "expert opinions" from people who are not experts.

There comes a time, however, when you have done enough research. It is time to make up your mind and make a decision. Acknowledge that research cannot answer every question. Some questions cannot be answered until you actually commit to a business and do it. It's a simple fact that the last piece of the getting into business puzzle, namely "How are you actually going to do in that business," will only be answered when you have actually worked the business.

Answer: Clearly focus on your goals as you built them in your business plan and researched them and have faith in your own judgment. These are the best tools to avoid the indecision that can come from over-analysis.

Conclusion:

After you finish the research, review the data, and ask yourself these questions:
1. Do I still want to go into business for myself?
2. Have I discovered what it takes to be successful in this business, in terms of others who have already done this business, and in terms of opportunity in my marketplace?
   a. If so, do I fit the business?

      b.   Am I like the people who have already succeeded in it?

      c.   Do I know what the successful owner does?

      d.   Can I do, or learn to do, what the successful owner does?

      e.   Do I want to do what the successful owner does?

3. Assuming I succeed in this business, will it allow me to reach the personal, professional and family goals that I need from my business?

4. Is this the best business I have found to help me achieve my goals?

If the answer to all the above questions is "yes," then move forward with your investment. If the answer to even a single one is "no," then it is not the business for you. Only if the answer is "I don't know," should you do more research. Knowledge of yourself, your goals, and your priorities is critical to making a good decision.

---

9 Reasons to buy your franchise

1. Fulfillment – it's a great feeling of satisfaction owning and operating your business.
2. Balance – Once the business has been tweaked and it's running smoothly, it's your decision how to put some balance in your life.
3. Independence – No boss to explain what you're doing and why.
4. Control – It's your responsibility so you get to make the decisions.
5. Financial security – when you get to be successful, the financial rewards and security is yours.
6. No more job layoffs.
7. Money – it may be the root of all evil but it beats the heck out of the alternative – not having enough.
8. Proven system/formula – let someone else invent the wheel – you'll just learn what road to follow.
9. Success – knowing you have made it.

Passion - Good Or Bad?

As a Business Broker I keep hearing buyers reacting to something they have been told by family or well meaning friends, if they intend going into business ownership make sure you: "Find your passion!" Focus on what you're passionate about and your likelihood of success increases.

I have thought a lot about "passion" and here's what I've come up with: After a short period of time the passion we had for something starts to slide. We need to look no further for this than our spouse or significant other or even our immediate family and friends. To re-invigorate these critical relationships that sustain us through life we celebrate birthdays, anniversaries, and special occasions such as Thanksgiving and Christmas, other important events such as Easter or July 4th plus ones that are important to us individually such as graduation from college etc.

So this lack of passion we often experience in life with the job we have been doing leads us to ask "There must be more?" The answer comes back "Let me buy a business of my own and do it my way."

Roadblock or reality?
If that's the place in life where you are at, my advice to you would be "Don't dwell on passion or it will become a roadblock for you." And here's why. There are so many different types of businesses you can choose. In the end your decision will boil down to three main things which all come together in one final question. The three things are: 1) amount of money you have to invest, 2) the lifestyle you want this business to create for you and 3) your perception about whether you have the skill to be successful. If your answer to all three is yes, then your final question will be: When I weigh these three things together, do I feel ready to take the financial AND emotional risk? Taking the financial risk is both an emotional and logical decision however taking the emotional risk is probably the hardest because there is no logic to it. Questions race through your mind such as "What will I do if I fail? What will I tell my family and friends if I fail? What will I tell the employees or …? What will I do? How will I recover from that lost money? How will I repay any debts I may have?"

So passion's nice but it's not critical. Consider some current business owners. The Dollar Stores owner that has to receive, unpack and store items on his shelf day in day out. The Fantastic Sam, Great Clips or SportClips hair salon owner – how many ways can you do a hair cut? The MAACO or Meineke auto mechanic - how many ways can you tighten the same nut?

I'm sure you get the point. Again, passion is good but not what this is all about. It's all about living your life with passion with your family, friends and things that are important to you (lifestyle), by finding the right business that will provide the means for you to do that.

Passion is more about what you are being (**business owner**), than it is about what you are doing.

Jargon And Buzzwords

There are different professionals that may participate in the process of buying a franchise. Some of them have a direct influence such as the franchisor, business broker, franchise consultant or business coach while others have an indirect role such as attorneys, accountants, financial planners, landlords, and property managers.

Each group of professionals tends to have its own business jargon and methodologies. If these terms seem confusing, stop and ask for a clear explanation. Don't let the jargon used exclude you from understanding what's happening – there is no such thing as a stupid question. This is your life and business – make sure it ALL makes complete sense to you. This is your responsibility. As I mentioned earlier, don't forget the glossary of terms at the back of this guide as it may assist you.

Write down industry jargon or buzzwords you want to research and better understand.

End Of Chapter Notes

Use this page to write down notes, ideas and other brainstorming for buying your franchise.

Section Two

Education

"*Be curious always! For knowledge will not acquire you, you must acquire it.* "

Dr. John G. Hibben

Introduction

The purpose of section two is to introduce some of the peripheral topics all small business owners will need to deal with when selling a business and I suspect almost without exception, areas we would prefer not to have to deal with as these topics are generally not part of our core competency. The topics I am referring to include tax planning and the tax consequences when selling a business, legal items including making sure all sellers are on board with the sale as well as the legal documents used in the sale, plus accounting and finance issues. In this section we also look at business valuations and their variations as well as the different professional services available for hire including those of a business broker.

What Is Franchising?

According to the International Franchise Association, franchises account for 40% of all retail sales in the US, franchise businesses were responsible for over $1.5 trillion in economic output and a new franchise opens every 8 minutes of every business day. The point here is that franchising is a major force into today's economy.

For clarity, in using the term franchise, I am not just referring to a business operating under a Franchise Disclosure Document (FDD) or previously called a Uniform Franchise Offering Circular (UFOC). This term includes corporations that license their brand or companies that own a trademark or patent and allow this to be used. For example, some oil companies license their brand. Companies that license their brand may have specific requirements so make sure you explore and fully understand their requirements.

There is no specific, all-encompassing definition of a franchise. Rather, it is a collection of attributes. Here are some key attributes that are common to most franchises:

1. Brand

In every franchise system the owner and developer of the system (normally called a franchisor) licenses franchisees to use trademarks, service marks, logos or advertising to identify and promote its business. In some franchise systems the franchise is only operated under the franchisors brand name, for example, Subway or Budget Blinds while in others the franchise brand name is used in tandem with a trade name, for example, Century 21/Bob Smith Real Estate.

2. Proven sales and marketing systems

This aspect not only includes putting together a palate of sales and marketing material to promote the brand and attract customers, but also analyzing and researching the demographics and site selection for the franchisee. This is an invaluable service that would take a business owner months and spend a considerable amount of time and money doing themselves.

3. Fees

In all franchise formats, the franchisor collects fees either directly or indirectly for the right to use the brand and participate in the system. The fees can include an initial fee, ongoing royalty fee, service fee, license fee or advertising fee. Other fees can also be charged but are explained in the Franchise Disclosure Document.

4. Training

The franchisor usually provides initial training to the franchise buyer once both parties sign the Franchise Agreement. Additional training may then be included on an ongoing basis by either the franchisor or at a local level near where the franchise is established. For more information, refer to the Franchise Disclosure Document.

5. Ongoing help

A key component of most franchises is the ongoing support provided by the franchisor. Ongoing support can be telephone, web-based, in-store visits or a mix of both. For specific details, look at the Franchise Disclosure Document.

6. Experience

One of the key ingredients that are normally provided by the franchisor is their business, management and specific industry experience. These are components they've learnt "at the coal face" and so bring these attributes to a system they have created and make available for others to invest in.

7. Efficiency and speed getting to market

One of the most attractive components of a franchise to a new franchisee is getting their business up and running in as short a time as possible. The franchisor has done the research to determine the demand exists, they have created trademarks and other copyrighted sales and marketing strategies and tested these in a local market and with their synergies and systems they've developed. Therefore, they can get a franchisee operational much quicker than the franchisee could on their own.

8. Culture

Each franchise has its own culture or a way of doing things. This is an inherent part of the system. The good news is that it doesn't require the franchisee to build and learn from their mistakes, because that's already been done for you as the franchise buyer.

9. Simplicity

This is not always true, but a franchise generally has a simple business model as it's been continually refined, picked over and redefined to truly polish it. How you determine if this is true is to ask the current franchisees – so don't forget to add this to your questions to ask when you do your research.

10. Limited independence

The franchise business model is most suited to a buyer from Corporate America that understands structure and following a process or set of instructions. They may possibly make great franchisees as their creative flair and personal drive should infect all those around them and raise everybody to a new level. A true entrepreneur like Donald Trump or Richard Branson would not be a good candidate as a franchisee.

Franchising:

A system that is designed to gain a disproportionate market share...and when done works exceptionally well.

Franchise Facts

According to the International Franchise Association (IFA):

- ✓ Franchising accounts for more than US$800 billion in annual sales and 40.9% of all retail sales.
- ✓ One in twelve business establishments is a franchise…and growing.
- ✓ A new franchise opens every 8 minutes of every business day.
- ✓ There are approximately 1,500 franchisors and 550,000 franchisees
- ✓ More than 8 million people are employed by franchises.
- ✓ Franchised businesses create more than 170,000 new jobs each year.
- ✓ According to the US Commerce Department fewer than 5% of franchises are terminated on an annual basis.
- ✓ In a study conducted by Arthur Anderson & Company, of 366 franchises, nearly 97% were still in business. In contrast, the US Small Business Administration revealed that 62.2% of all new businesses failed within their first 6 years.

Pricewaterhouse Coopers conducted a study for the IFA Educational Foundation to report the economic impact of franchising and provided the following data.

	From franchises	% of the Private sector economy	In franchised businesses (direct)	% of the Private Sector economy (direct)
Jobs	18,121,595	13.7%	9,797,117	7.4%
Payroll	$506.6 billion	11.1%	$229.1 billion	5.0%
Output	$1.53 trillion	9.5%	$624.6 billion	3.9%

Direct Employment by Economic Sector:

Durable goods manufacturing 10,335,000
Franchised Businesses 9,797,000
Financial Activities.. 6,826,000
Construction.. 6,826,000
Information 3,629,000

Note on the data: All data from 2001
The direct contribution comes from the franchised businesses while the "indirect" contribution reflects the additional jobs, payroll and output franchised businesses create such as food suppliers to restaurants.

Source: IFA Educational Foundation, Economic impact of Franchised Businesses, a study conducted by Pricewaterhouse Coopers.

Brief History Of Franchising

The word "franchise" derives from old French and means "privilege" or "freedom." In the middle ages a franchise was a privilege or a right and the local sovereign or lord would grant the right to hold markets or fairs, to operate the local ferry or to hunt on his land. With time, the concept extended to the king granting a "franchise" for different commercial activities including building roads and the brewing of ale. In essence the king was giving someone the right to a monopoly for a certain type of commercial activity. Over time the regulations governing franchises became a part of European Common Law.

Over the centuries the franchising concept has evolved as the economies of the nations of the world have evolved. In Germany certain major ale brewers granted franchises to certain taverns, giving those taverns the exclusive right to sell their ale. This was the beginning of the concept of franchising, as we know it today.

In 1851, the Singer Sewing Machine Company began granting distribution franchises for their sewing machines. Singer had written franchise contracts, which were the forerunners of modern franchise agreements. In the 1880's cities began to grant monopoly franchises to streetcar companies and utilities for water, sewerage, gas and later electricity.

Around the turn of the century, soft drink bottlers, the oil refinery companies and the automobile manufacturers began to grant the right to sell their products. At this stage in the evolution of franchising it was essentially just the granting of the right to distribute and sell a manufacturers products, today called "product franchises."

"Business format franchising," which is the dominant mode of franchising today, came into the economic scene after World War II with the return of the millions of US servicemen and women and the subsequent baby boom. There was an overwhelming need for all types of products and services, and franchising was the ideal business model for the rapid expansion of the hotel/motel, restaurant, automotive service, real estate brokerage, auto rental, and fast food industries.

During the explosion of the 60's and 70's there were many problems and some abuses in franchising. Some companies got into trouble because of poor management or lack of capital. But there were a few totally fraudulent franchise companies that literally took people's money and ran. Whatever the causes, the results were the same: a trail of failed franchisees who lost everything. Therefore, the need for regulation was inevitable, and has since helped provide potential franchise investors the information they need to make an informed and safe decision.

It became clear that the franchise industry had to change in order to remain a viable business concept. On the industry side, the International Franchise Association (IFA) was created with the specific intent of uplifting the professionalism of the entire industry. The IFA holds training in all aspects of franchising which greatly enhances the industry. Members of the IFA are required to adhere to the IFA's Code of Ethics, which sets a high standard. The IFA works closely with the US Congress and the Federal Trade Commission on improving how the industry relates to the franchisees.

US Laws And How They Regulate Franchising

A basic definition of a franchise, albeit a partial one can go like this: **A franchise is an investment in a long term (5 years to 25 years or more) business license.**
The licensor/franchisor grants you a license to distribute goods and services using his trademarks, trade names, trade styles and business systems. It is a complete system of doing business. Indeed, the word "system" is the key concept in franchising. A franchisee receives assistance with site selection, personnel training, business set-up, advertising, and product supply. The franchisor will have manuals and training in place to teach the systems to the new franchisee. In a nutshell, a franchisee is investing in a license that gives him access to someone else's expertise, experience, and method of doing business.

But a franchise is a special kind of business license, because during the term of the franchise, the franchisor has some control (which allows it to charge royalties) or provides significant assistance. So, "control and assistance" are what distinguish a franchise business license from all other business licenses.

What kinds of franchise regulations are in place?

Franchise regulations are in place for the benefit of the person considering buying a franchise.

Federal and state law in 14 states, including California, requires that a franchise buyer or prospective buyer receive a current copy of the document formerly known as the Uniform Franchise Offering Circular (UFOC.)   This is now called the Franchise Disclosure Document (FDD) and includes the following:

1. The FDD must be provided at the first meeting with a representative of the franchise company.
2. A current copy of the FDD must be in the possession of the prospect/buyer for 14 calendar days before the prospect may sign any commitment or make any deposits.   As the FDD is updated annually, the most up to date FDD must be provided.
3. The franchise contract, with all blanks filled in, must be in the possession of the prospect for five business days before he/she may sign it.
4. The law requires that almost the entire FDD be written in "plain English." The only exceptions are contracts and financial statements.
5. No money may be paid to the Franchisor until the buyer/prospect has a copy of the FDD.

In my opinion, you do not need an attorney to read the FDD for you; unless there is some term you do not understand, however, I do strongly recommend that a qualified franchise or business attorney be retained by you to explain the franchise contract and any other legal document, such as a lease, loan documents or similar that might be included. You may also wish to have an accountant review the three years of audited financial statements from the franchisor.

Today, franchising is a highly regulated industry, which offers a great opportunity to those individuals who truly want to realize their dream and go into business for themselves.

For more information visit my website: http://www.Andrew-Rogerson.com. On the left hand menu choose "Franchising" and go to the bottom of that page and click on the link called "The Federal Trade Commission Consumer Guide to buying a franchise" where you can get a copy of the document on franchising issued, naturally enough by the Federal Trade Commission.

Ethics And Culture

A couple of very important points I would like to make here.

First, in the previous topic it was explained that a franchise was an investment in a long term business license (generally 5 years to 25 years or more.) This is an important point to remember as you work through your decision making process. Buying a franchise should not be seen as a short term option. As the franchisee, there are many skills, experience and nuances you need to learn to truly maximize your return on investment. And this is part of the investment you have with your franchisor that they will provide this for you. So don't look for immediate gratification or readily accept the negative comments from some people you may hear as your franchise is part of the economy that constantly ebbs and flows and reacts positively when you invest your time and energy into it.

Second, the International Franchise Association has a Code of Ethics. If you would like to read the Code of Ethics go to the following address: http://www.franchise.org/industrysecondary and you will be able read this first hand.

From my perspective, dealing with ethical business people is now an important business requirement. Over the last few years in particular, there has been critical media focus on sales tactics and techniques that hurt parties in a transaction. As you move through your business ownership search you will come in contact with many types of business people. Make sure you feel comfortable with their ethics and how they represent themselves. If you do not, obviously move on and look for an opportunity somewhere else. Just as importantly, though, remember your experience as when you open your business, customers that come to you will have the same concerns and so it will be your opportunity to show your ethics and values.

Finally, an item that is not talked about too much but is an extension of the above comment, every franchise has a culture or way of doing business. This culture is invariably set by the owner or the corporate or head office as this is the place where the ideas, training and processes are rolled out. Make sure you try to early on determine the culture of the franchise and whether or not you see yourself fitting into that culture.

Who Buys A Franchise?

The IFA conducted a 20-year study on the "typical franchise buyer" and here are their conclusions.

Buyer	Amount	Comment	Additional Comment
Cash Available	Under $120,000		The typical buyer has under $120,000 though finance is generally available if the buyer qualifies.
Net worth	$250,000 to $600,000		Net worth is important but a cash deposit is what the franchisor needs.
Average Income	$65,000 to $150,000		All buyers look to make at least what they currently make…but they all hope to make more.
IRA/401K		Yes – most have	Most have IRAs or 401Ks but almost all don't want to take the penalty and use them. Other options are available; if the buyer is interested.
Average Age		35 to 50 years old	Most franchisors are careful with the age groups they work with.
Gender/couple		Male/Couples/Female	Women have a higher success rate but the percentage of ownership follows this order.
Owned Businesses		Most have not	Most buyers have not owned a business before; but this is changing. 30% have owned a franchise before and are now buying their second because of the ongoing training, marketing and support.
Work experience		Corporate	The vast majority of franchise buyers come from a corporate environment.
Corporate position/title		Mid Management or above.	Downsizing, reduced promotion prospects, political work environments, constantly changing and increased corporate pressures are encouraging buyers to have more control of their life and make more of their own decisions.

Why Buy A franchise?

If you've decided that business ownership is right for you or you simply want to know more so you can make an informed decision, this guide is for you. In simple terms, there are three options to business ownership available to you and these are:
1. Start your business from scratch.
2. Buy an existing business (either a privately held business or franchise.)
3. Buy the rights to a franchise and open it from scratch.

Option one of starting your business from scratch is without doubt the hardest. Not only do you have to come up with the idea, you have to research and spend time to make sure there is a market for your idea. Once you establish there is a market – if in fact there is a market, you have to take the idea that's been a dream, take action and convert it to a viable business by successfully executing all the main components of a business such as the sales and marketing, financial controls, operations, training, human resources and management. All on a shoe string budget. Do you have all the necessary skills, time and money to support yourself until your idea turns a profit?

Option two and three are where most potential business owners are at. Applying previous business experience (and probably management experience), buying an existing business and building on its success or turning it around is a good option. If it's an existing business it has a footprint in the business world and a history of performance so you can see what it's done. By bringing your own energy, time, money and experience your goal is to take it to the next level.

Option three complements option two in that you are taking an existing idea that a franchisor has created and tested and once again bringing your energy, time, money and experience. Some of the main reasons business owners choose the franchise model include:

1. A franchise comes with a known name and therefore brings instant recognition.
2. Brings a proven product or service.
3. The franchisor provides ongoing support. This means you are in business for yourself but not by yourself.
4. The franchise comes with an operating system. All the mistakes have been made and the kinks ironed out.
5. Training is included by the franchisor to get your business up and running in the quickest time possible.
6. Finance is readily available as the business model has been proven.

What Types Of Franchises Are Available?

One of the interesting things about franchising is that there is a broad range of franchises available. This is part of the reason I use the consultative process as we need to understand your interests, business strengths and weaknesses, management skills, financial capacity and risk tolerance to find the right match for you. Also, we need to make sure when we find a good match that the franchise is available where you live.

However, to answer the question – What types of franchise are available? There are three parts to it.

Part one is deciding whether you want to be a single Unit franchisee or an Area Developer that owns two to six units. Next is the Master franchisee that owns a territory and brings on board the single unit franchisee or area developer. Page 42 explains the different types of franchise ownership formats.

Part two looks at the different industries to find the right fit for you. Some of the major franchise industries include (and they are changing all the time): Advertising/Marketing; Animal/Pet related; Automotive; Business Services; Computer Services; Dry Cleaners/Laundries; Education; Fast Food; Financial Services; Health and Beauty; Home Services; Home Based; Hotel/Motel; Internet; Manufacturing; Medical Services; Recreational; Restaurant; Retail; Route Delivery; Senior Care/Health Care; Service Businesses; Sports/Fitness and Tax Preparation.

Part three is for you to decide what category of business you like such as retail, business to business, residential or personal services, home based etc.

If you would like to get a feel for some of the options, please go to my website: http://www.Andrew-Rogerson.com and click on the "Franchises" tab from the menu on the left hand side. Once this page loads you will see towards the bottom an option called "If you would like to see the list of current franchises we have available, please click here."

Below is a screen shot of the part of the website that has the link you can choose to see the different franchise options available. This link is highlighted with the red arrow.

Questions?

If you have questions, please allow me to be of service to you by offering a process I use that puts you in control to see if franchising is the right option for you - all at no cost to you whatsoever. For more information, please call me on ▾ **(916) 570-2674** ◎ or click here to complete a request for me to contact you.

If you would like to see the list of current franchises we have available, please click here.

If you would like some more information about buying a franchise, the following articles may be of interest to you.

FDD And Other Transaction Documents

Franchise Disclosure Document

As I have mentioned before, any franchise you consider buying must first be properly disclosed to you through the Franchise Disclosure Document (FDD). The FDD is prepared by the franchisor and must be submitted to the Federal Trade Commission (FTC) for review and approval before any franchises are sold and then annually updated. In addition, many states also require a copy of the FDD so they too can review and approve it. For example, I am in California and the Department of Corporations must review and approve the FDD.

All franchise purchases must have an agreement signed between the franchisor and franchisee. If a Master franchise or Regional Director's franchise is being purchased, the FDD will include this document if the buyer is also purchasing these rights.

The FDD purely by its size can appear an intimidating document. However, the FDD is your friend as its main purpose is to explain and inform you as much as possible about the franchise and what you can expect from making your investment in it. Also, the good news is that the format of the FDD is exactly the same with each franchise you consider buying. That is, it's laid out the same, regardless, so this means you can clearly see what each section covers.

There are currently 23 sections of the FDD. Very briefly, here's what each covers.

1. The Franchisor, its predecessors and affiliates

This section tells you the legal entity that owns the franchise, how long it has been in business and its location; which may or may not be important to you. If the entity is fairly new the franchise may not be well established. If the legal entity does not mirror the brand you are buying then you may be speaking with a Master who is licensed by the Franchisor.

2. Business Experience

This section introduces the individuals behind the franchise and their business and management experience. This information is helpful as it gives you can idea of the management stability of the organization. If you see a lot of turnover or lack of education by the key management this could be a red flag.

3. Litigation

Any lawsuits between the franchisor and franchisees, or franchisor and regulators are required to be declared in this section.

4. Bankruptcy

Bankruptcy disclosures apply to the franchisor, its affiliates, officers and managers but not to individuals who serve as a franchisor's outside directors. The disclosure is only required if the bankruptcy occurred within the last 10 years.

5. Initial Franchise Fee

The estimated initial investment and all fees, including the initial franchise fee, on-going royalties, advertising fees, site fees, transfer fees, etc. This also includes a disclosure by the franchisor if they require the franchisee to buy any initial property, goods or services to open the business.

6. Other Fees

Any recurring and occasional fees must be reported in this section so the franchisee knows up front what these costs may be. Examples include royalty fees, advertising fees, reservation fees, training fees, transfer fees, interest or late payment fees, software fees, rent etc.

7. Initial investment

This section provides a snapshot of the initial fees or costs the franchisee should expect to pay to get this franchise up and running. If you were to start your own business, this would include looking at leasing a location, security deposits, fixtures, furniture and equipment, leasehold improvements, initial inventory etc. The same applies to your franchise but instead of you doing all the work to collect the data and hopefully get it right, the franchisor will do that for you and tell you what's included. Just remember, this section does not detail any loan servicing costs or salary you need as an owner.

8. Restrictions on sources of products and services

This section explains what products must be bought from the franchisor or what minimum standards need to be followed when sourcing supplies, inventory, products or brands. It also covers any restraints on the sale of products and services. One of the key ingredients of a franchise is its ability to provide a consistent experience to all customers that patronage the franchise anywhere. To ensure the consistency and quality is met, this section outlines those requirements.

9. Franchisee's obligations

This section gives an overview of the franchisor's obligations, the franchisee's obligations, and where they are found in the franchise contract.

10. Financing

If the franchisor has an in-house franchising program, this would be explained here. Different models are used by different franchisors but read this fine print to understand the costs if you decide to use a program sponsored by the franchisor. Financing may include equipment leases or promissory notes or security guarantees etc. If the franchisor does not have any in-house finance but leaves that to third party lenders, no disclosure is required.

11. Franchisor's obligations

This can be the most detailed item in the FDD. It describes what the franchisor is required to **do** for their franchisee, for example, training requirements, advertising obligations, site selection, pre-opening obligations, ongoing obligations once the franchise is up and running and the time frame from signing the agreement to the business being open and operational. This is an important part of the FDD so study it in-depth and ask plenty of questions.

12. Territory

The territory restrictions of the franchisor are explained in this part be it with just the franchise brand or any other brands owned by the franchisor. Not all franchises have a territory restriction so read this section carefully if this is important to you.

13. Trademarks

The franchisors words and symbols used to identify franchised outlets is a definition of a trademark. The United States Patent and Trademark Office is the place to register the trademark but trademark rights are said to be incontestable after six years. This section describes what trademarks the franchisor owns and how, as the franchisee, you can use them.

14. Patents, copyrights and Proprietary information

Other forms of intellectual property such as patents and copyrights are defined here with an explanation of how the franchisee can use them. Examples of these items include marketing plans, market research, customer lists, recipes and formulas etc.

15. Obligation to participate in the actual operation of the franchise business

So you're buying your franchise to have your neighbor work in it as manager while you retire to another part of the country? Not so fast. The franchisor may have requirements that the owner of the franchise work in it or at least participate in its management; this is the place in the FDD where this is explained. Active involvement of the owner of the franchise equals a greater chance of success.

16. Restrictions on what the franchise may sell

Similar to some earlier items in the FDD, the focus here is on explaining whether the franchisees are restricted to selling only items approved for sale by the franchisor or if the franchisee is restricted from selling to certain customers or outside their territories etc.

17. Renewal, Termination, Transfer and Dispute Resolution

An explanation of what happens if the franchisee decides to leave the franchise earlier than the expiration of the franchise including termination, and transfer. This section also deals with the process for resolving a dispute between the franchisor and franchisees. For this reason, this is a good section to discuss with your attorney.

18. Public figures

Public figures are used by some franchisors to raise the profile of the business and are part of its sales and marketing plan. The purpose of this section is to explain the relationship between the franchisor and the public figure so the franchisee knows its duration and what has been agreed to and the extent of the involvement of the public figure.

19. Earnings claims

Most franchisors choose not to make earnings claims. However, if they chose to do so, this is the section in the FDD where this is done. Only one in four franchisors publishes any sales or earnings claims but it's important to read this section so you understand the financial data the franchisor provides and whether you feel the franchisor has the financial resources to be successful.

20. List of outlets

This is a wonderful section for you as the franchise buyer. It discloses, by state the last three years history of open/closed units, plus, three years of new unit openings. The information not only shows the name, address and phone number of the current franchisees so you can give them a call, but also by state, the details of all franchisees that left the franchise system in the last year, for whatever reason be it failure, sale, retirement so you can also contact them.

21. Financial statements

This includes 3 years of audited financial statements of the franchisor including balance sheet so the buyer can look for trends in the business be they up or down. This is a good section to discuss with your accountant or attorney as it reveals the financial depth of the franchisor including the revenue and expenses. If this is a relatively new franchise system, it will indicate if the franchisor is relying on capital from franchise fees sold to franchisees etc.

22. Contracts

The goal of the FDD is to inform. If the buyer likes what they see and wishes to buy a franchise, there is a need to enter into contracts. This section provides, up front, a copy of any contracts including the Franchise Agreement, leases, and any other documents a franchisee is asked to sign.

23. Receipt

The FDD normally includes two copies of a receipt of the FDD. One copy of the receipt is to be signed by the prospective buyer and returned to the franchisor, so the franchisor has evidence for the regulators that they have complied with the disclosure regulation. The remaining copy is kept by the prospective buyer.

Franchise Agreement

A copy of the FDD will also include the Franchise Agreement. Both the franchisor and you would sign when you are ready to buy your franchise and the franchisor or Master Developer is willing to have you join their franchise system. And as we mentioned above, a prospect or buyer must be given a copy of the Franchise Disclosure Documents before they make any deposits. If you prefer to have more information, please speak to an attorney that specializes in business law.

Additional documents

The purchase of any franchise involves a number of different documents, depending on the type of franchise you buy. For example, if your franchise is run from a retail location you will need a lease or if it is a restaurant that serves alcohol, you will need a license in order to do that. The franchisor will explain these to you as part of their requirement.

Sources of additional information include:

www.ftc.gov   On the Home Page there should be a Quick Finder box that goes to a section on "Franchises & Business Opps."

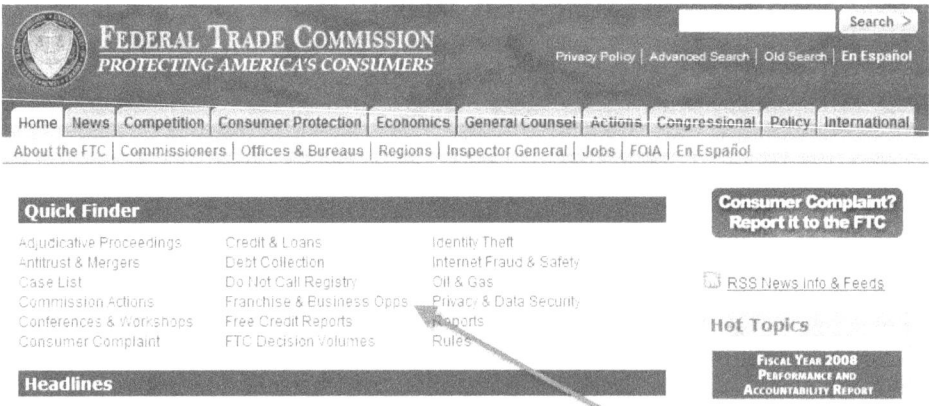

Other websites include:
www.business.gov
www.findlaw.com
www.lawyers.com
www.copyright.gov
http://www.businesslaw.gov

Franchise Ownership Formats: Unit, Area Developer & Master

There are different franchise formats because the different formats meet different needs of the franchisor. Because franchising is an entrepreneurial concept, the descriptions below may vary with different franchisors. However, the description below will give you a basic understanding so you can get specifics from your franchisor. Bottom line: ask questions and be clear what is being offered so you can decide if that works for you.

In simple terms there are three franchise formats. These are a Unit franchise, Area Developer and Master franchise (sometimes called sub franchising.) As the name suggests, a unit franchise is one franchise owned and operated by a franchisee. This is normally their sole business. An Area Developer is someone that chooses to have more than one franchise in the same unit. Their goal may be to build out a local territory with 3 to 6 units. Reason for doing this is that an individual unit may take about the same amount of work as 3 to 6 units as the Area Developer has hired out the management of each location. By doing this, the Area Developer is leveraging his management skill and creating a higher income than operating one franchise unit.

Although they are not a franchise format per se, it's worth noting that some unit franchises are part of a franchise system because they initially started as an independent privately held company in one city. However, the product or service being offered was also sold in a similar way in other cities across America. For a variety of reasons such as buying power, consistency of branding, sales and marketing synergies, ability to work with similar minded business owners etc, the owners of the independent privately held companies decided there was value in moving their business into an existing franchisors model. Also, to entice them to join the franchise, special conditions or exceptions were granted which may or may not continue.

Master franchise (or sub franchising)

Master franchises really exist so that individuals or corporations can buy the rights to sub-franchise within a specific U.S. territory or another country. The initial franchise fees are higher but a master franchise license can lead to greater growth than a traditional franchise. By paying the higher fee, the master franchisee takes on more responsibility which then allows them to keeps a good portion of the initial fees and royalties that the individual franchisees pay over time.

Franchise companies generally communicate with their franchisees directly or through a master franchisee. A master franchise allows the franchise company to expand in a specific territory, often a major market or in one or more states.

A master franchise essentially runs two separate businesses — one operating a single franchise and the other expanding the franchise company. Each requires different skills and, generally, the companies are set up separately. For both, having sales and management experience is a definite plus for a prospective master franchisee.

The types of master franchise opportunities available are as varied as the people who run them. From discount golf retailers to skincare centers, master franchises are everywhere. But before you close a deal for purchasing a master franchise, it's important to have a clear understanding of exactly what's involved. You must remember, for instance, that no matter how attractive an opportunity appears, the business viability of the entire system must be solid.

Here are some points to consider before making your final decision about which format of franchise is right for you:

What are your responsibilities?

A master franchise generally has two responsibilities. The first is to operate a unit franchise in the territory that belongs to the master franchisee. Secondly, recruit and support individual or unit franchisees on an as-needed basis.

Do your research.

As a master franchise buyer, you will be working with two different entities – the franchisor or "home office" and the master territory or organization. For you to be successful as the master franchise it's important for you to make sure that the franchise system is based on a solid business model. Without a viable business model, it's unlikely that a master franchise could succeed. You will also need to research the market and territory demographics. Make sure that the territory has a population that can support your projected sales.

Consider a road trip or two.

There's nothing better than doing your own research to gather market intelligence with actual visits to as many franchise locations as possible. If you detect any problems, cross this franchise off your list. Don't be tempted to rationalize red flags. If you sense trouble, regroup and consider another franchise system; it's as simple as that.

Look for the right match.

Even if the business model is solid, you'll want to make certain that the franchise suits your investment limitations and your goals. If you don't have the capital, then it's not a good match. If you're not interested in the business, then it's not a good match. Be prepared to walk away if the opportunity doesn't feel right.

Pick one approach.

Becoming a master franchiser versus buying one franchise isn't necessarily a better or smarter business move. What's important is that you choose either approach for the right reasons and with careful consideration. Running a master franchise requires a different set of skills than owning one franchise. The skills for building strong sales, for instance, are not the same as those needed to operate the business successfully.

Interview successful master franchises.

If possible, try to talk to other people in the master franchise field. Find out, for instance, what kinds of challenges they face, what kind of support is available, and if they had to do again, what they would do differently. If speaking with other master franchise company owners isn't possible, search the Internet, go to the library, and do whatever you can to immerse yourself in the language of a master franchise. The more you know the better off you'll be.

Remember, a franchise is not a dealership or distributorship. These formats are often used by manufacturers or suppliers of products. No separate fee is charged to a dealership or distributor with the products being supplied at a wholesale price where the manufacturer takes their full profit and doesn't look for ongoing royalties.

Benefits Of Franchising

As I write this, this is an interesting question. It depends on whose perspective I use. If I ask a franchisor they will have a different perspective to a franchisee. If I ask a brand new franchisee or one that has been following the system for a long time or one that just left, I expect I will get a different answer. I guess the same could be said if I asked some of the customers or employees or suppliers. However, this guide is about helping inform a potential buyer so I have written this topic from this perspective and in general terms the benefits of franchising are:

1. The FDD gives a comprehensive outline for a buyer/investor on what to expect when buying a franchise. This includes an estimate of starting costs, a description of the competition, initial start up training, a national advertising plan plus access to similar small business owners who are working in the system. If you were to start your own business from scratch you would not have this road map. Similarly, if you were to buy an existing business it's unlikely you will also get such a road map.
2. Instantaneous goodwill. This is a wonderful asset and not very complicated.
3. Start up assistance. The franchisor will work with you to find the right location, negotiate a lease, bring on board best prices with suppliers, computer and software systems, initial training and other benefits in a very short period of time that are hard to quantify or qualify unless you try doing all this on your own. So many startup businesses go broke simply because they don't have the resources to turn these things on quickly and so waste time and working capital not to mention the human capital from all the stress and strain.
4. Some franchisors assist with finance, ongoing business plans, employee training manuals, access to the right fixtures, furniture and equipment, merchandising, pricing, employee relations and other demands that can wear down an independent small business owner not to mention the help that may come from a master developer or other franchisees in the system.
5. Some franchisors assist with the business resale. When the franchisor decides they need to retire or move on, the franchisor can assist with finding a replacement.

The above are just a few of the many benefits. The real answer to this question comes from the skills and energy you bring as a franchisee and how you can use the others around you to get up to speed as quickly and professionally as possible.

The perfect franchise to buy:

The perfect franchise to buy is one with the following attributes:

1. Has been established for three years or more
2. A reasonable price
3. A reasonable down payment (hopefully about 30% of the full price)
4. Approved for third party financing
5. Reasonable sales by the current franchisees (hopefully increasing each year)
6. Positive feedback from existing franchisees
7. Meets your personal goals and compliments your personality and the skill set you bring
8. Good and attractive location (if important for the business type)

Downsides Of Franchising

As we mentioned in section one, franchising is not for everyone. Business ownership is not for everyone so it stands to reason franchising is not for everyone. As you work though your process to decide if buying your franchise is right for you, bear in mind the franchisor also wants the right fit. The strength of their franchise comes from successful franchisees so part of their process is to make sure you are a fit for them. My own personal experience has been looking at buying franchises. On one occasion I did all the due diligence and was almost convinced I had found the right match. However, the franchisor had a final questionnaire they required completing and the nature of the questions was enough to convince me that buying this particular franchise was not right for me. So here are six things to consider when deciding if franchising is right for you.

1. Franchise standards may not be universally successful.
2. Independence is restricted. The best buyer is some-one from Corporate America that understands structure and how to use it.
3. Franchisor controls key assets such as brand name, systems, hours and days of operation and National advertising can reduce your profitability.
4. Franchisor ownership and management will change.
5. The conduct of other franchisees can affect the brand and therefore your business – this is good and bad.
6. Internet strategies may impact the success of the system.

How do millionaires get to be millionaires?

According to the book, The Millionaire Next Door – five out of six millionaires acquired their wealth through business ownership.

How Much Does A Franchise Cost?

First, what do you pay for the license? It takes two forms. First, there is an "initial franchise fee". The initial franchise fee for a single unit franchise can vary but is usually in the $20,000 to $30,000 range. This is what you pay for the license, the training, and for getting into the system.

Secondly, almost all franchises charge on some ongoing basis, oftentimes called a royalty, and this is typically in the range of 4% to 7% of sales. Additionally, some franchises charge a mandatory marketing fee to cover the costs of nationally promoting and marketing the franchise so it grows. There is considerable variation, however, so when you are looking at a specific franchise, make sure it's clear on what you will be required to pay.

Finally, there may also be the investment to open the business, whether it is franchised or not. If it is a retail business, it will need inventory, shelving and cabinets, cash registers and so on.

Below are the results of a survey by the Franchise Times that shows the range of costs associated with starting a franchise and how it relates on a percentage basis.

Costs	Percentage
$50,000 or less	28.6%
$50,001 to $100,000	23.9%
$100,001 to $250,000	32.7%
$250,001 to $500,000	9.2%
More than $500,000	5.6%

Random Q & A

Question: Does buying a franchise require a unique set of skills?

Answer: You should expect the franchisor to provide the vision, tools and training. However, if you are buying a market-specific business, such as an automobile lube and tuning, it is good to have an appropriate background. There are hundreds of different kinds of franchises, and some do require training in the given area. That is one reason why fast food franchises are so popular; the skills required are very trainable.

Finance Options

With all the items on the checklist to take care of, often a key component of the deal is you securing financing.

Most franchisors have a process in place for securing a loan for the buyer. This is the normal process but as a business broker I do have contacts with national, regional and local lenders who will finance a franchise purchase to a qualified buyer.

To make an application for a loan, you will normally need:

✓ An application form from the lender you will need to complete.
✓ Proof of an acceptable amount as a downpayment including proof if it is in cash (* See **Note** below.)
✓ A minimum credit score acceptable to the lender (this varies but is about 680 on the FICO and up.)
✓ Supporting documents for the loan such as tax returns, payroll stubs to show previous wages and income, business plan plus many other documents as they relate to the transaction.

Finance may also be required for funding working capital or Accounts Receivable or assets of the business such as vehicles or office equipment. In some cases, financing can be provided by the franchisor but in most cases it will be provided by a third party.

To minimize frustration, early in the process disclose to the franchisor you will need finance and that it will be a condition on which to make your purchase. The franchisor can then explain their arrangements so you can do the appropriate research to see if the finance is acceptable to you at the right terms and conditions.

Consider securing funding for the downpayment from different sources such as family, friends, banks or credit unions. These are not necessarily typical sources of funds for every buyer, but other options include:
✓ Home equity loan
✓ Local banks
✓ Small Business Administration (SBA)

If your money is in a 401k plan and would like to use this as downpayment to buy a business, more information is available from companies that specialize in this sort of funding. More information is available in Section 8 called "Other finance options."

* **Note**: If a downpayment is not readily available it is one of the first things I would get in place before talking to franchisors. Otherwise, you may waste a lot of time and energy and create a lot of frustration not only for yourself but also for others.

Sources of additional information include:

SBA Loan program: http://www.sba.gov
Small Business finance: http://www.vfinance.com
Finance options: http://www.business.com/Finance.asp
CNN Money: http://money.cnn.com/index.html
Federal Government Small Business Finance: http://www.business.gov/guides/finance

Professionals You Can Hire

One of your many decisions is what professional help you will need, if any to buy your franchise. At a minimum you will need the services of a business broker or franchise consultant to help you find what franchises are for sale and explain the franchise buying process. They should also be able to assist with finance, help answer roadblocks about the process, assist with your business plan and consistently and professionally meet with you to help you narrow down the franchise opportunities that make the most sense to you. This service will ensure you don't waste time and money looking at the wrong opportunity. Too many franchise buyers simply burn out as the process is more complex than they expected and was hard working through all the variables in some sort of reasonable order.

Although this may not be obvious or your choice, you may also have family and/or close friends that want to follow what you are doing…and give well meaning advice. My suggestion is that you handle family and friends early in the process by letting them know what you are doing and clearly explain the boundaries that make sense for you. I do know some buyers that never told their family and close friends as they simply didn't want their input or the frustrations they expected by unwanted help. You may want to involve family and friends every step of the way…or you may not. Clearly indicate what you want and stick with it. If your need changes, let them know but also let them know if it's temporary help you seek or longer term help.

Attributes

In a moment we will look at the different type of professionals you can hire. However, here are some thoughts on the type of attributes you may look for in that professional.

Accreditation

If you are looking for a professional with a specific skill set, then their accreditation will tell you the education they have obtained for that specialized skill. There are literally hundreds of three and four letter accreditations. To see if that accreditation is what you are looking for, simply do a Google search. Another option is to find their website and read about their education levels to make sure their academic expertise is what you want.

Compensation

Is the advisor being compensated by commissions on the sale or are they charging you a fee for a service? Some advisors have a combination where they get a fee for a certain part of their time but also can get commission if they make a sale. Fully understand how they are compensated to make sure it makes sense to you.

Business knowledge and experience

Going to college, reading and passing the courses and networking with small business owners are nice. However, when the rubber hits the road, it is experience that counts. Look for someone who understands the dynamics, pressures, stresses and responsibilities that business ownership demands. This should be one of the foremost skills you need from any small business advisor. The best way of finding that person probably comes from networking with other small business owners who have "been there and done that."

Expert network

A good advisor should have a strong network of accountants, attorneys, consultants, lenders and other specialists they can refer to you. Referrals are the main stay of most advisors because the work they do often permeates into other disciplines. Their work is therefore exposed to other professionals that get to know not only the advisor's professional work, but also their reputation.

Goal and style synergy

You may meet many advisors but what you are looking for is *the right one*. If honesty and trust are important to you, that will be the type of advisor that will work best for you. Similarly, as you work with an advisor you will build a relationship, and so it is important the person you are dealing with understands what you are about and is able to communicate clearly. As mentioned earlier, if the advisor just wants to use buzzwords and jargon to inflate their importance, then that may not be the type of advisor you want working with you.

Reputation and references

As a business owner you value word of mouth and your reputation. It is therefore rewarding to thank professionals you think highly of by using their services again or referring them to somebody you know that needs that same service. However, a lot of the work the advisors do is highly confidential so they have to be careful when handing out references. If a referral is given unsolicited from a "happy customer" that you know professionally, that should give you encouragement to further inquire about using that professional's services.

Random Q & A

Question: Why should I consider franchise ownership as an attractive option?

Answer: Three good reasons.
1. The franchise business model lets you be in business for yourself without being by yourself.
2. The franchisor provides a tested and proven base structure for the business thereby allowing you as the franchisee to drive the operational wheel. This should be your key strength making you attractive to the franchisor to let you buy the franchise.
3. Franchisors provide the guidance, innovation and marketing materials they test and prove on a regular basis.

Types Of Professionals To Hire

A lot of franchise buyers are reluctant to hire professionals. Reasons include their belief that the cost is too high, the professional doesn't know as much about their business choices as they do, or the buyer cannot readily find the right person or someone they know used that service and had a bad experience.

If the right professional is hired for the right reason, the value they bring should far outweigh their cost. This value will be in saving you time, not only in terms of hours spent but giving back your time so you can spend it on more profitable areas. The two primary important reasons though to hire a professional are because of the expertise they bring to solve a problem and providing an impartial perspective to an unexpected situation. The tax, finance, accounting, legal, human resources and business laws are complex. The right professional can quickly navigate you through these areas.

Here are some thoughts on each of the different types of professionals you may need to hire, how to find them and most importantly, knowing if they are the right fit for you. I've also included blank templates so you can write down questions that come to mind that you may want to ask each of these professionals.

A Word of Caution

Accountants, attorneys and tax advisors training and core competency is to protect and therefore advise their clients about minimizing financial, legal and tax risks. Similarly, they don't want to give "risky" advice—such as encouraging you to buy a franchise —and lose a customer or generate negative word of mouth because something went wrong in the deal.

Buying a franchise does come with risk. Assessing risk is one of the most important tasks you have to perform. It is therefore important that you find an accountant, attorney and/or tax agent that understands the risk you are taking and offer advice accordingly. Some of these professionals offer such conservative advice that they may hold you back from "living your dream."

Bottom line: Make sure you have people on your team who will give you good advice on how best to buy your business—not just to protect you from a mistake they feel is important to them.

Accountant/Tax Advisor

There are three types of accounting professionals a business owner may consider hiring to assist with the sale of the business. These are a Certified Public Accountant (CPA), tax attorney or a personal financial planner. The option chosen will likely come down to cost and the specifics you need to address.

The above list is not to suggest that others can't assist. For example, there are many street-wise and highly skilled bookkeepers that may have intimate knowledge of a business and can readily advise you. However, if you are looking for a professional to hire and you have no existing relationships, then these are the professionals to consider.

Resources for Locating CPAs:

American Institute of Certified Public Accountants	http://www.aicpa.org
Thomas Financial	http://www.thomasonfinancial.com

Tax Attorneys:

Lawyers.com	http://www.lawyers.com
National Association of Enrolled Agents	http://www.naea.org/MemberPortal
Findlaw.com	http://www.findlaw.com

Sources of additional information include:

National Association of Financial and Estate Planners	http://www.nafep.com/index.html
Risk Management Association	http://www.rmahq.org/RMA
Walker Advisory Associates	http://www.waa-online.com/new/waaonline

Write down Accounting/Tax Questions you want to research or ask.

If you have any accounting or tax questions you have been thinking about or they come to mind as you read this guide, write them down here so you can research them at the appropriate time.

Attorney

Just as there are specialists in finance and accounting due to the breadth of the subject, so too are there experts in the different fields of law. It is important that you find an attorney that specializes in the specific area of law you need, in this case, business law. Your attorney will not only be able to guide you through the legalese of buying your franchise but also help create your legal entity such as a corporation, company or partnership.

Resources for Locating Attorneys:

The American Bar Association: http://www.abanet.org
Your state's Bar Association: http://www.abanet.org/barserv/stlobar.html

Sources of additional information include:

http://www.abanet.org/public.html
http://www.legalzoom.com
http://www.nolo.com
http://www.lesi.org
http://www.bizfilings.com
http://public.findlaw.com

Legal Questions to Research

If you have any legal questions you have been thinking about or they come to mind as you read this guide, write them down here so you can research them at the appropriate time.

Business Broker/Business Consultant/Franchise Consultant

Business brokers, also known as Business Intermediaries, provide a range of services to help buyers and sellers enter and exit business ownership respectively. There are also business consultants and franchise consultants you can choose if just buying a franchise is the current direction you are choosing to go. The best reason to use a business broker to buy your franchise as opposed to a business consultant or franchise consultant is that a business broker has a much better knowledge of the buying and selling process; not just franchises. This advantage can be tremendous as you can engage the services of a business broker to help you find a business for sale or a franchise or both. As you work through your business ownership options it's good to work with the one consultant so they get to know what is and isn't working for you but most importantly, develop a level of trust so you know your interests are being looked after. If you don't think this is happening, regardless of who you are working with, look for a new broker/consultant. Your broker/consultant plays a critical role in being a sounding board for you as well as understanding all the processes, forms and relationships you may need.

The International Business Brokers Association (IBBA) is a global organization and has the largest membership of business brokers in the United States. It provides a forum for the industry including education standards for business brokers to obtain accreditation with the designation of Certification of Business Intermediary (CBI).

Sources of additional information include:

International Business Brokers Association   http://www.ibba.org
Murphy Business and Financial   http://www.murphybusiness.com

Business Broker/Consultant questions to research

If you have any questions regarding business broker/consultant you have been thinking about or they come to mind as you read this guide, write them down here so you can research them at the appropriate time.

Personal Financial Planner

Earlier in this section we discussed whether hiring an accountant or tax advisor was necessary. We mentioned that a personal financial planner may be an option that works for some sellers, especially if the planner you are considering hiring is experienced in advising on financial statements. Specific skills or characteristics to consider when looking for a personal financial planner include the following:

Accreditation

There are literally dozens of three and four letter accreditations. These include specializations such as CLU (Chartered Life Underwriter) for life insurance or QPA (Qualified Pension Administrator) for business retirement and benefit plans. Investment advisors must register with the Securities and Exchange Commission and become RIAs (Registered Investment Advisors). Advisors with more sophisticated training include Certified Financial Planners (CFP) and ChFC (Chartered Financial Consultant).

Compensation

When hiring a financial planner, there are three compensation options available. First, they can be compensated by commissions on the sales of investment and insurance products. Second, they can be fee-based only or third, they can charge you a fee for a service but also can get commissions for products they sell.

Sources of additional information include:

Certified Financial Planner Board of Standards   http://www.cfp.net
Chartered Financial Consultant   http://www.chfc-clu.com

Personal Financial Planner questions to research

If you have any questions regarding personal financial planning you have been thinking about or they come to mind as you read this guide, write them down here so you can research them at the appropriate time.

End Of Chapter Notes

Use this page to write down notes, ideas and other brainstorming for buying your franchise.

Planning

> "Being busy does not always mean real work. The object of all work is production or accomplishment and to either of these ends there must be forethought, system, planning, intelligence, and honest purpose, as well as perspiration. Seeming to do is not doing."
>
> *Thomas A. Edison*

Introduction

Sections one and two cover a lot of the basic terms and concepts that come up when selling a privately held business. The focus of section three is three-fold. First, it is to look specifically at your business to see if you can uncover any areas that need improvement prior to listing it for sale that should return a higher selling price, or in other words, a simple return on investment. Second, develop a plan so you can build a clear direction and strategy to sell the business. Third, identify any professionals you may want to hire to help with the sale and determine what you can expect those professionals to provide. This will lead you to the ultimate goal of successfully selling your business for the best price with as little stress and frustration as possible.

Just a Reminder

This is a workbook. It is meant for writing, scribbling and making notes. It requires you making notes, finding, reading and writing questions, along with reminders and inspirations about documents or processes. Staple into the pages any notes you take or articles you read. By the time you finish this section you will have available any information a buyer or professional you hire may need. The remaining sections of this book then capture the flow of the transaction and the best practices to follow. Now, let's do some research!

Importance Of A Business Plan

This is one of the smallest topics in this guide but probably the most important. In my opinion, one of the most important things a new or potential business or franchise owner needs to do is write a business plan (and create a budget.) Once again, in my opinion, the business plan becomes the road map for the new business owner as it forces questions which therefore create or force answers. And it's through both the questions and answers you will be able to determine whether it makes sense to buy a franchise or more importantly, which franchise to buy.

Not everyone will agree this is the way to go but it's easy to see if this makes sense by looking at the questions below. All these questions should be typical to most business plans, and that's one of the points. Each business will have things that are unique to its business so a good plan has to be flexible. You can start with a core document and then simply add or remove items as they apply to your business and make sense to you. And remember, one of the best things about a business plan is that it records where you are at, at a certain moment. A business plan is a living and breathing document and needs to be revisited and updated so its stay fresh but keeps you focused and accountable on what needs to be done in the short term and what can and should be moved into the long term.

Within a good business plan is a good budget that also keeps you focused and accountable. If the business is doing better than expected you can ramp up the growth strategy you devised for the business. If the business is not growing as fast as anticipated, you can see the weaknesses and implement solutions to turn things around.

Most business plans have complementary documents attached to them. For example, a good business plan also needs a good Sales and Marketing plan.

Which business plan do I use?

There are many software programs available that have different Business Plan templates. And the best news is that they are free. Simply search the web and you choose the one that works for you. There are a couple of alternatives. First, the cheapest option is if you have Microsoft Word. They have a great suite of business plans and they are free. They have business plans for starting new business, an established business or just a general business plan. Simply open Microsoft Word, go to "New" and search using the keywords "Business Plan" and the options will be made available to you. The second alternative is to discuss this with your business broker or consultant and see what they use. They may have an option to share with you and if you follow this option and have questions about how to get it completed, they could readily assist you with that.

Importance Of Your Business Plan

If the above section on the importance of a business plan makes sense to you, it will have more meaning as you work with and create your own business plan. A business plan forces discipline and accountability; which what a business is all about. It allows you to be creative and write down what you are thinking so you can come back to it at any time and see if you are going in the direction you planned. If you've wandered off track, the business plan will allow you to see that.

The biggest complaint I hear about a business plan is that you have to keep it up to date. Absolutely – that's its primary purpose. If your business plan is out of date it means you have started in a different direction that you planned. But, it means your business plan must be brought up to date so you are forced to consider the direction you are drifting in case that direction is wrong.

Random Q & A

Q: How important is it for new business owners to work with a mentor like SCORE as they explore franchise opportunities?

A: It couldn't be more important. By working with SCORE counselors who have "been there done that," you can potentially avoid many of the mistakes that we all made. SCORE's resources are outstanding whether you work with a counselor one-to-one, through a workshop, or via the Internet with online counseling through SCORE. Their website is http://www.SCORE.org.

Finance Planning Tools

The axiom goes: If you can't measure it you cannot manage it. And so it is with the importance of making financial tracking tools, such as a cash flow forecast or pro forma for the business and just as importantly, your personal life.

Whether you buy the rights to a franchise, start a new business, or buy an existing business, means you will be taking on risk as you plan, open and get your business functioning and part of the economy. Our goal in this topic is to introduce some financial planning tools that may be helpful as you work through your decision making process. If financial planning is not one of your primary skills there may be value in engaging a professional to do this for you. However, your franchisor should have a lot of systems in place so it's important to understand those systems then find out what you need additionally in your own right to understand the financial performance of your business, and then how this impacts your personal tax and financial planning situation.

If you engage a professional, the plan should be to make it a long term relationship so you get to know each other, define what help you need, on what basis and frequency, how the data can be collected then moved into a reporting frequency and cycle. Once all this is in play, the data needs to be thoroughly interpreted and analyzed so it gives you a road map of where your business has come from, where it is now, and where it is going.

Below I've touched on some financial tools made of Excel spreadsheets or Word documents you may find useful for your business. The type of business you build and the industry will determine the final make up of the financial tools you need.

Each of the tools described below is from an Excel spreadsheet or Word document put together by SCORE. You can download these files from my website at http://www.Andrew-Rogerson.com. Once this page loads, on the left hand side there is a menu of options. Towards the bottom choose the option called 'Sample Documents' and you will see different Word and Excel files. Please select the document you need.

Start Up Expense Planner

As you start planning your new business opportunity with the purchase of your franchise, it will be a good idea to know what your initial out of pocket expenses will be so you can make sure you have cash available to cover those costs. The spreadsheet below gives you an example to follow. Obviously change the columns to suit your needs.

Item or Service	Quantity	Budget	Actual Cost	Variation	Date bought
Computer(s)	2	$1,000	$700	$300	
Printer - Color Laser	1	$350	$300	$50	
Monitor	2	$350	$400	-$50	
Software (s)	2	$600	$500	$100	
Desks	2	$500	$550	-$50	
Chairs	2	$200	$150	$50	
Fax machine	1	$200	$150	$50	
Phone	2	$200	$150	$50	
Telephone lines	2	$100	$120	-$20	
Filing cabinet - 4 Door	1	$50	$80	-$30	
				$0	
Website Design	1	$600	$600	$0	
Website hosting - 12 months	1	$100	$80	$20	
				$0	
Business cards		$100	$100	$0	
Flyers		$300	$300	$0	
				$0	
Business License		$50	$100	-$50	
Legal fees - to create entity		$500	$1,000	-$500	
Accounting advice		$1,000	$1,200	-$200	
				$0	
Marketing consultant		$500	$400	$100	
Insurance - Business		$400	$350	$50	
Insurance - Auto		$500	$600	-$100	
Total costs		$7,600	$7,830	-$230	

If you would like a template created in Excel to use for your business to track your start up expenses, please go to: http://www.Andrew-Rogerson.com. Once this page loads, on the left hand side there is a menu of options. Towards the bottom choose 'Sample Documents'. After this page displays, look for document # 9. Simply download, complete, save, and monitor it to make sure you are staying within your budget. This tool has been created by SCORE.

Personal Budget Planner

As you begin your journey to buy your franchise, you may like to review your current personal spending to see if you can make any cutbacks. If you are currently single and have no other responsibilities, it makes sense to see where your current expenditures go and if you can make any cutbacks in the short-term. Conversely, if your family currently has two incomes and will drop to one when you start your business, you may want to do the same by seeing what you can cut back, so you can fund your new business until it becomes profitable.

To help you do that, review the spreadsheet shown below or if you prefer, create your own in Excel and do some "what-if" scenarios. The choices are all yours, however, I would suggest that starting a new franchise generally costs more and takes longer than most business owners starting out expect, so discretion is the better part of valor.

	A	B	C
	Main Item	Current Amount	Revised amount
1			
2	Allowances - kids		
3	Auto - Insurance		
4	Auto - gas		
5	Cash		
6	Charitable contributions		
7	Childcare		
8	Clothes		
9	Education		
10	Entertainment		
11	Gifts		
12	Groceries		
13	Hair care		
14	Household costs		
15	Insurance - House & contents		
16	Insurance - Medical		
17	Medical and dental expenses		
18	Miscellaneous		
19	Pet		
20	Property taxes		
21	Rent Mortgage		
22	Repairs and maintenance		
23	Taxes		
24	Travel		
25	Utilities - Cable		
26	Utilities - Cell		
27	Utilities - Electricity		
28	Utilities - Gas		
29	Utilities - Internet		
30	Utilities - Phone		
31			
32	Total Per Month		
33	Variation		

There is no specific spreadsheet on my website for this but just copy the layout above into Excel and thereby create your own.

Profit And Loss Projection

A Profit and Loss Projection is a planning tool to track your projected sales against your costs to run your business and therefore show how profitable you will be. Below is a very basic P&L projection

	Jan-08	% B/A	Feb-08	%	Mar-08	%	Apr-08	%	May-08	%	Jun-08	%
Revenue (Sales)												
Category 1	5,000	27.8	5,500	29.7	6,000	30.0	8,000	33.0	12,600	43.3	21,000	53.2
Category 2	10,000	55.6	10,000	54.1	11,000	55.0	13,000	53.6	13,000	44.7	15,000	38.0
Category 3	2,000	11.1	2,000	10.8	2,000	10.0	2,000	8.2	2,250	7.7	2,250	5.7
Category 4	1,000	5.6	1,000	5.4	1,000	5.0	1,250	5.2	1,250	4.3	1,250	3.2
Total Revenue (Sales)	18,000	100.0	18,500	100.0	20,000	100.0	24,250	100.0	29,100	100.0	39,500	100.0
Cost of Sales												
Category 1	2,500	50.0	2,750	50.0	3,000	50.0	4,000	50.0	6,300	50.0	10,000	47.6
Category 2	3,000	30.0	3,000	30.0	3,200	29.1	3,600	27.7	3,600	27.7	4,000	26.7
Category 3	1,000	50.0	1,000	50.0	1,000	50.0	1,000	50.0	1,100	48.9	1,100	48.9
Category 4	100	10.0	100	10.0	100	10.0	120	9.6	120	9.6	120	9.6
Total Cost of Sales	6,600	36.7	6,850	37.0	7,300	36.5	8,720	36.0	11,120	38.2	15,220	38.5
Gross Profit	11,400	63.3	11,650	63.0	12,700	63.5	15,530	64.0	17,980	61.8	24,280	61.5
Expenses												
Salary expenses	2,000	11.1	2,000	10.8	2,000	10.0	2,000	8.2	2,000	6.9	2,000	5.1
Payroll expenses	1,500	8.3	1,500	8.1	1,500	7.5	1,500	6.2	1,500	5.2	1,500	3.8
Outside services	300	1.7	300	1.6	300	1.5	300	1.2	300	1.0	300	0.8
Office supplies	100	0.6	100	0.5	100	0.5	100	0.4	100	0.3	100	0.3
Repairs and maintenance	50	0.3	50	0.3	50	0.3	50	0.2	50	0.2	50	0.1
Advertising	120	0.7	120	0.6	120	0.6	120	0.5	120	0.4	120	0.3
Car, delivery and travel	80	0.4	80	0.4	80	0.4	80	0.3	80	0.3	80	0.2
Accounting and legal	500	2.8		0.0		0.0		0.0		0.0	500	1.3
Rent	400	2.2	400	2.2	400	2.0	400	1.6	400	1.4	400	1.0
Telephone	50	0.3	50	0.3	50	0.3	50	0.2	50	0.2	50	0.1
Utilities	45	0.3	45	0.2	45	0.2	45	0.2	45	0.2	45	0.1
Insurance		0.0		0.0	400	2.0		0.0		0.0		0.0
Taxes (real estate, etc.)		0.0		0.0		0.0		0.0	400	1.4		0.0
Interest	250	1.4	250	1.4	250	1.3	250	1.0	250	0.9	250	0.6
Depreciation	300	1.7	300	1.6	300	1.5	300	1.2	300	1.0	300	0.8
Total Expenses	5,695	31.6	5,195	28.1	5,595	28.0	5,195	21.4	5,595	19.2	5,695	14.4
Net Profit	5,705	31.7	6,455	34.9	7,105	35.5	10,335	42.6	12,385	42.6	18,585	47.1

for 6 months using the sales numbers above from the One Year Sales forecast spreadsheet.

If you would like your own working document so you can do your own projections, please go to: http://www.Andrew-Rogerson.com. On the left hand side there is a menu of options. Towards the bottom choose 'Sample Documents'. After this page displays look for documents #11 & #12. Download the spreadsheet to your computer and use it. This tool has been created by SCORE.

Other Finance Planning Tools

In addition to the Startup expense spreadsheet, the Sales forecast spreadsheet, and the Personal Budget spreadsheet, a good thing to do before starting your business is to create a Profit and Loss projection for the first year and the first three years. You can also create a cash flow projection so you can understand when you will have to make the actual payments to keep your business open and in good graces with your suppliers, lender and employees. Good business practices may also include doing a competitive analysis and/or breakeven analysis. If you would like to do these there are spreadsheets available. Finally, if you want to create an initial balance sheet and ongoing balance sheet these documents are also available.

All these documents give you reference points as your business builds, and a financial road map to know you are heading in the right direction or make some adjustments to get to your destination.

Cash flow projection

If you would like a working document, please go to: http://www.Andrew-Rogerson.com. When this page loads, on the left hand side there is a menu of options. Towards the bottom choose the option called 'Sample Documents'. After this page displays look for document # 13 & #14.

Breakeven Analysis

If you would like a working document, please go to: http://www.Andrew-Rogerson.com. When this page loads, on the left hand side there is a menu of options. Towards the bottom choose the option called 'Sample Documents'. After this page displays look for document # 15.

Competitive Analysis

If you would like a working document, please go to: http://www.Andrew-Rogerson.com. When this page loads, on the left hand side there is a menu of options. Towards the bottom choose the option called 'Sample Documents'. After this page displays look for document # 16.

Balance Sheets

If you would like a working document, please go to: http://www.Andrew-Rogerson.com. When this page loads, on the left hand side there is a menu of options. Towards the bottom choose the option called 'Sample Documents'. After this page displays look for document # 17 & #18.

Financial Projection Models

If you would like a working document, please go to: http://www.Andrew-Rogerson.com. When this page loads, on the left hand side there is a menu of options. Towards the bottom choose the option called 'Sample Documents'. After this page displays look for document # 19 & #20.

If this is all new to you, SCORE provides a great source of information and help. To find a local SCORE chapter go to their website http://www.score.org and search based on your zip code.

Establish Your Preferences – The Consultative Approach

The franchise buying process is a consultative process. You have questions and you need answers. To get those answers you must have a consultant that can introduce you to the franchises that are available in your area, be a guide to assist you through the process and help with questions about finance, legal processes to follow (notwithstanding they cannot give legal advice – that is the role of an attorney) and simply be an independent sounding board for the many questions or road blocks you may encounter.

With the work of your consultant you can then cut loose and focus on the franchise opportunities that make the most sense to you and the consultant from the franchisor. Remember, the franchisor has put together a system that is unique to the franchisor. The franchisor will have competitors so they don't want to disclose their FDD and other supporting material if they aren't sure the buyer has the capacity to buy the franchise. A good consultant will provide an introduction to the franchisor and establish your bona fides for you including your financial position, business and management skills and reasons why you have an interest in their particular franchise. Additionally, by working with a consultant you may find starting a business from scratch or buying an existing business better suits your needs so make sure you have a qualified consultant that has the skill and resources to help you with that.

To help with the above process, below is the Buyer Qualification Profile I use. The information in the profile allows me to quickly get an understanding and suitability you will have for either an existing business for sale or franchise. The Buyer Qualification Profile allows me to schedule a meeting with you and go through a series of consultation questions. My process is that ALL information given to me is totally confidential. You get to choose what information you want me to release be it to the owner of a business, another broker whose business we have found that has a listing for sale that appeals to you or the franchisor of a franchise that brings a match to your interests.

The Buyer Qualification Profile may trigger questions for you as you complete it. These questions, when combined with the business plan we've talked about, should give you a solid foundation to build your process and arrive at point to make your ultimate decision about whether or not you will buy your business or franchise.

So let's take the next steps and take a look at the questions asked in the Buyer Qualification Profile.

Buyer Qualification Profile

CONFIDENTIAL

The more we understand your needs, wants, goals and values, the better we will be able to assist you.

Contact information

Name	
Address	
City, State, Zip	
Home Phone	
Office Phone	
Cell	
Fax	
Email	

Instructions: This is a type on document. First save to your computer, fill in your information and return via email. You can also print and fax it to:

OFFICE:

NAME:
ADDRESS:
PHONE:
CELL:
FAX:
WEB: www.Andrew.Rogerson.com

PERSONAL and BUSINESS INFORMATION

Name _____   Date of Birth _____

Address: _____

City: _____ State _____ Zip _____

U.S. Citizen ☐ Yes   ☐ No

☐ Own   ☐ Rent   How long? _____

Telephone Numbers: Home (   )   Work (   )

Cell (   )   Fax: (   )

Email: _____

Best time to call: _____

Education: ☐ High School ☐ Bachelors ☐ Masters ☐ PhD ☐ Other

University or College(s) Attended   _____

Major(s) _____   Year Graduated _____

Employment: Current occupation   _____

Type of Business _____

Title/Position _____

Length of Employment _____   Salary_____

Responsibilities: *(attach resume if available)* _____

Professional affiliations _____

Previous employment _____

Type of Business _____

Spouse's Current Employment _____

Type of Business _____

Title/Position _____ Length of Employment _____ Salary _____

Have you ever owned or operated a business?

☐ Yes   ☐ Full-time   ☐ Part-time   ☐ No

If yes, explain _____

What attracts you to owning your own business now?_____

What did you like MOST about your past job or business_____

What did you like LEAST about your past job or business?_____

What do you consider your GREATEST achievement? _____

On the basis of your work experience, your strengths are?_____

Your weaknesses are?_____

Would you enjoy owning a business where you:

Consult ☐   Sell   ☐   Market ☐ (check all that apply) your product or service?

How do you rate your sales ability? Weak ☐ Average ☐ Strong ☐ Very strong ☐

Why are you considering a change from employment at this time?

_____

_____

In terms of purchasing a business or franchise I am: ☐ Mildly Interested
☐ Very Interested ☐ Ready To Purchase

Do you have any experience in: ☐ Advertising/Marketing ☐ Public Relations
☐ Sales ☐ Management ☐ Customer Service ☐ Finance

Will you devote full time to your business?   ☐ Yes   ☐ No

How would you rank your family's support of starting a new business?
☐ Fair ☐ Medium ☐ Good ☐ Very Good
Explain:_____

Will family members be involved with you in the business? ☐ Yes ☐ No
Whom: _____

How would you rate your following business skills?

Sales	Average ☐	Good ☐	Very Good ☐	Excellent ☐
Management	Average ☐	Good ☐	Very Good ☐	Excellent ☐
Organization	Average ☐	Good ☐	Very Good ☐	Excellent ☐
Financial	Average ☐	Good ☐	Very Good ☐	Excellent ☐
Marketing	Average ☐	Good ☐	Very Good ☐	Excellent ☐
Customer Service	Average ☐	Good ☐	Very Good ☐	Excellent ☐

Rank the most important starting with 1 and the least important 10

Control My Future   ____
Build a Business   ____
Personal Growth   ____
Flexible Time   ____
Family Involvement   ____
Community Involvement   ____
Income Level   ____
Build to Sell   ____
Be My Own Boss   ____
Other   ____

Please select the attributes that best describe you.

Amiable	☐	Reliable	☐
Controlling	☐	Competitive	☐
Independent	☐	Hard Working	☐
Outgoing	☐	Results Oriented	☐
Flexible	☐	Money Oriented	☐
Diplomatic	☐	Risk Taker	☐
Persuasive	☐	Open Minded	☐
Leader	☐	Intuitive	☐
Direct	☐	Considerate	☐
Growth Oriented	☐	Understanding	☐
Loyal	☐	Spontaneous	☐

How long have you been researching business and franchise opportunities?
_____

How will you know when you have found the right business?
_____

In what geographical area would you like to operate your business?
_____

How soon do you want to start this business?_____

Whatever success you have enjoyed in your past business experience, many people are looking for something different and better; please share the three most significant "changes" that you would like to overcome by owning your own business, being your own boss:

     1. _____
     2. _____
     3. _____

What business categories do you have an interest in? _____

What kind of business hours are you interested in?
Part-time ☐   Full-time ☐   Management ☐

Is the opportunity to have a multiple unit operation important to you?
Yes ☐   No ☐

Daily roles you would enjoy:

Managing Employees	Yes ☐	No ☐
Sales prospecting	Yes ☐	No ☐
Marketing	Yes ☐	No ☐
Networking	Yes ☐	No ☐
Customer Service	Yes ☐	No ☐
Providing service quotes & estimates	Yes ☐	No ☐

Please describe below the most important things to you in choosing a business
(These can include but are not limited to money, success, lifestyle, learning, challenge, fun, personal satisfaction, achievement or anything else that you think is important):

_____

_____

_____

_____

_____

Have you ever been convicted of a felony?   ☐ Yes   ☐ No
If yes, explain: _____
Have you ever filed bankruptcy?   ☐ Yes   ☐ No
Have you ever been an officer in a company that has declared bankruptcy?
☐ Yes ☐ No
Cash Available for investment in a business $
Do you have a source for additional funds without obtaining a business loan?
☐ Yes ☐ No If yes, please explain:

_____

Monthly household overhead: $ _____

How will you cover your monthly living expenses as you build the business?

_____

Do you want to supplement or replace your current income? _____

Business Characteristics

My ideal business would look something like this: (check most appropriate answer in each case):

Proven, easily replicated system	☐ important	☐ somewhat	☐ don't care
Recognized business or franchise brand	☐ important	☐ somewhat	☐ don't care
Potential for significant growth	☐ important	☐ somewhat	☐ don't care
Potential for longevity of the business	☐ important	☐ somewhat	☐ don't care

Image of business interested in   ☐ professional ☐ don't care

(check all that apply)   ☐ automotive ☐ retail food ☐ service business services ☐ home/personal services

Business location is based at   ☐ store ☐ home/office ☐ commercial office
☐ calling on customers in their business or
☐ calling on customers in their home

Business environment   ☐ casual ☐ suit and tie ☐ don't care

Competition would be   ☐ high ☐ moderate ☐ low

Customer type desired   ☐ repeat ☐ businesses ☐ general public ☐ don't care

Employee type desired   ☐ blue collar ☐ white collar ☐ skilled ☐ don't care

Number of employees   ☐ 10+ ☐ 5-9 ☐ none to 4

Product versus service   ☐ products ☐ services ☐ both

Your cash investment level   ☐ $100k ☐ $50-99k ☐ $25-49k

Maturity of business   ☐ a mature, well-established business w/strong support and structure
☐ a young, developing business w/good support, but more flexibility
☐ a ground floor opportunity, offering the highest potential reward or risk

Who will make decision (check all that applies)   ☐ me ☐ spouse ☐ other

Management style   ☐ actively involved in all aspects of the business
☐ develop employees & delegate responsibilities

Timeframe for being in business   ☐ 3 – 6 mos. ☐ 1- 3 mos. ☐ now

Timeframe for deciding   ☐ 3 – 6 mos. ☐ 1- 3 mos. ☐ now

Growth   ☐ multiple units ☐ prefer one unit if same monetary success is possible

Your need for personal income   ☐ 1+ year ☐ 6 – 9 mos. ☐ 3 – 6 mos.

Hours of business   ☐ prepared to work whatever hours needed to launch the business
☐ willing to work nights & weekends as retail may require
☐ only interested in traditional business hours

Preferred roles in the business   ☐ customer service
☐ management of staff
☐ management of operations
☐ prospecting for business, sales of product or service
☐ marketing, networking, developing referral sources

		Risk/Opportunity	☐ want to 'cherry pick' locations or markets by being among the first in my community to open the business

Risk/Opportunity   ☐ want to 'cherry pick' locations or markets by being among the first in my community to open the business
☐ prefer to wait until others are already in business in my market to benefit from their experience

Income   ☐ goal is make the maximum income possible
☐ seeking to grow and sell business
☐ plan to slow down when goals are met

How do you want your family and friends to perceive your business?
         ☐ Contributes to society
         ☐ My business' tangible assets exhibit my financial success
         ☐ My previous experience was a key factor for entry and success
         ☐ I don't care

FINANCIALS

ASSETS			*LIABILITES & NET WORTH*	
Cash In Banks (itemize)	$		Notes Due Banks and Others (itemized)	$
	$			$
	$			$
Marketable Stocks & Bonds	$		Taxes Payable	$
	$			$
Life Insurance Cash Surrender Value	$		Loans	$
	$			$
TOTAL CURRENT ASSETS	$		*TOTAL CURRENT LIABILITIES*	$
	$			$
Real Estate Owned	$		Real Estate Mortgages	$
Other Assets	$		Other Liabilities	$
	$			$
Retirement Accounts	$			$
IRAs	$		*TOTAL NON-CURRENT LIABILITIES*	$
401k	$		*TOTAL LIABILITES*	$
TOTAL NON-CURRENT ASSETS	$		*NET WORTH*	$
TOTAL ASSETS	$		*TOTAL LIABILITES & NET WORTH*	$

SOURCE OF ANNUAL INCOME		ESTIMATE OF ANNUAL EXPENSES	
Salary		Mortgage Payments	
Bonus & Commissions		Automobile Payments or Lease	
Dividends		Insurance Premiums	
Other Income		Other Expenses	
TOTAL		TOTAL	

I certify that the information I have provided on this application is complete and correct. I authorize the release of this information to obtain verification of any of the above information. The purpose of this questionnaire is to compile general information and is not binding upon either part.

THIS IS NOT A CONTRACT

Yes I agree ☐ Name: _____

Name: _____ Phone: ( ) _____

What You Will Need To Buy Your Franchise

If you are serious about buying a franchise there are five things you will need to move through the process. You don't need to provide these to everybody that asks, but when you get to a point where it will support your request for more information or show you have the ability to buy the franchise it's good to have things ready. If there is more than party that wants to buy that one franchise, by having these documents ready it will give you an edge.

The documents you need are:

1. Resume

A resume is now an important component for three reasons. First, your resume talks about your industry experience. Second, your resume talks about your business and hopefully management experience. There are many buyers that would like to buy a franchise but they simply don't have the requisite skills or ability. Your resume will help address that issue with a franchisor. Finally, most franchise buyers need to borrow in order to buy the franchise. A lender will not consider offering you a loan to buy the franchise without seeing your resume. Up until recently, credit was freely and readily available and a lot of time was given to buyers who weren't successful. As a result, the availability of finance has tightened and so franchisors are reluctant to spend too much time with would be buyers until they know that a buyer would qualify for finance if they chose to buy a franchise.

It's also worth considering having different resumes for different franchises, in case you want to highlight a skill that is important to one franchise but not important to another.

2. Personal Financial Statement

The need for a Personal Financial Statement mirrors the reason you need a resume. Most franchisors require the buyer to have a minimum net worth and available capital as a downpayment to buy a franchise. They also require this to be disclosed up front as they don't want to invest the time qualifying, educating and revealing confidential information to a buyer that is not qualified.

3. Copy of your credit score

Yes – you guessed it. The same reason you need a credit score is outlined above. My suggestion is that you pull your credit score and have it available to provide when you feel comfortable providing it. If your credit score is pulled too many times in a short period of time, it can lower your score. Plus, if you supply your credit score when you feel comfortable providing it, it puts you in control.

4. Proof of downpayment

This is important to have when it's needed so you can assure a franchisor and/or a lender you have the downpayment in cash and ready to go. As I have mentioned previously in the guide, lenders are more careful in approving loans and they want to make sure the source of a downpayment is from a readily identifiable source and not coming from a source that is being used to collateralize the loan. For example, if the downpayment is coming from equity in your home, that equity may already be used to approve the loan in the first place – and so it can't be counted twice.

5. Agreement with your significant other or partner

This last one was thrown in for good measure. It's probably the most important but the least obvious. How does your wife, husband, significant other or partner feel about you buying a franchise? The industry you've chosen? Will they work in the business with you? Have you discussed the financial and emotional risks you are taking? The questions are endless. Make sure your partner travels with you on all aspects of this journey. Yes – two heads are better than one, and if you both work through the many variables it will help you both once you get into the actual process of opening and running your franchise. Also, as a business broker when I am consulting with buyers I ALWAYS like the partner to attend any consultations so I can make sure their needs and concerns are addressed and understood. If they aren't on board with you, your chances of success are greatly diminished plus it adds a great stress on your relationship.

6. Completing the Buyer Profile Questionnaire

It's important that when you start the process to buy your franchise you have as much information as possible and can determine the direction you want to go as soon as you. Franchisors will be spending time and resources explaining their business models, your consultant will be making available their time which will probably be outside regular business hours plus there is the time and expense you will be incurring travelling, making phone calls and other activities to move through the process. The Buyer Profile Questionnaire in conjunction with this guide should enable you to answer a lot of your questions and feel confident (albeit nervous) about the direction you are going. If you're direction isn't making sense, make sure you discuss this with your consultant. If it still doesn't feel right then take a break from the process as buying your franchise is not the right place for you…at the moment.

Random Q & A

Q: Is it also helpful to visit other franchisees as well?

A: Absolutely. Make arrangements to visit their locations and examine their processes. Ask them if they would buy the franchise again, if the franchisor is providing enough support, if the experience is living up to their expectations, and if they are meeting their business goals. These relationships will also be helpful should you decide to move forward with the franchise purchase. You can develop a network of friends that have the same base knowledge and abilities. It's a good feeling to know that you can call any of them with questions or good ideas to share.

How Do I Know Which Franchise To Buy…And Why?

Many of the calls I get are from individuals who know they want to buy a business but are just unsure how to find the one that would be the best fit for them. It's not uncommon for a client to tell me they have been looking for a business for years and just "can't find that right fit". Some say they have looked at hundreds of businesses and none seem to be the right one! So if you are feeling overwhelmed or unsure about the best way forward, you are not alone. Many of my buyers come from corporate America and have not purchased a business before. They are not sure of all the choices and how to best leverage their skill set in their own business.

So how do you find the *RIGHT franchise*?

The process I use with my clients is a consultative process that assists clients with looking at not just what the business does – but what they want the business to do for them. What are your personal goals? Why do you want to go into business in the first place? Where do you expect to be in five years? What do you expect business ownership to do for you personally, professionally and financially? It's critical to look inward and determine what's important to you. We keep track of all this with a business plan. The business plan allows you to record your personal and business goals and where you're at and add and remove questions as you research the variables that are important to you. We then bring it altogether as a road map of your personal and business interests to the business or franchise that provides the right match. This is a proven formula and if followed will allow you to be successful.

Once we are able to identify your goals, the next question is how do you want to go about achieving them? Through our consultative process, we discuss the various characteristics and preferences you want in your own business. Do you want a retail business? Do you want an outside sales or service business? How large of a sales component do you want? Do you enjoy working around equipment? Does the image of the business make a difference to you? These are examples of the many preferences and characteristics you want to consider. We also look at not just what the business does, but the role you play in the business.

Now you've identified your goals and the characteristics and preferences you want in your business, I look at making recommendations of business opportunities that might be a good structural fit based on what you have told us during the modeling process.

Whether you are looking for an existing business or a new franchise, I am able to help you find the right fit safely and affordably. My process "reverse –engineers" the method many people go through, turns abstract thoughts into focused vision and helps you reach your goals! And the good news is that there are well over 120 high quality prescreened franchise companies available. My goal is not to have you check or validate any more than one or two at a time so you don't waste time or try to process too much information.

How much does it cost?

There is no charge for the consultation process. I am paid by the franchisor if there is a match. And that's important to note. Your ability to buy a franchise has to work not only for you, but also the franchisor. The franchisor's success comes from having strong and successful franchisees. They therefore have their own validation process to make sure you will meet their needs and be part of their successful system.

My main focus is to work with <u>Qualified Candidates</u> who want to make it to the finish line.

Who is a qualified franchise buyer?

Below is a list of items I look for when trying to help buyers. Not all the items need to be present but if some are missing then it may not be worthwhile investing the time and energy to buy a business or franchise.

1. <u>Motivation:</u> Motivation to find the right business. On a scale of 1-10, this should be 9 or 10 with a conviction and desire to own a business.
2. <u>Time to do the Research:</u> This is critical. Finding the right business opportunity takes time and research. Plan to dedicate 6-8 hours per week for 6-8 weeks to do the research.
3. <u>Time to be in Business:</u> The ultimate goal is to be able to make a decision in the next 60-90 days and be in business as soon as possible thereafter.
4. <u>Finance:</u> In general terms, for a franchisor to invest their time to work with you and qualify you, you will need a minimum of $50,000 in liquid capital, home equity, 401K funds or other source of equity. Most franchisors are also looking for a net worth of $150,000 or greater and good credit; especially if financing is required. Some franchisors will require more that this but this is a good start to look at various opportunities.
5. <u>Living Expenses:</u> Part of your plan should be to have put aside money to cover your personal living expenses for 6-12 months. Getting your business established takes time and so you need to include this in your plan.
6. <u>Spouse/life partner:</u> If married or you have a life partner, both need to be in agreement with the decision to buy or open your own business, and willing to attend the consultation appointments and work through the process.
7. <u>Financial partners:</u> If a financial partner is involved, it is critical that all the financial partners be willing to attend the consultation appointment and be involved in the process.

Both 6 and 7 are important as a lot of work can be done by a lot of people in the process only to find that one spouse/life partner or financial partner who hasn't attended the meetings is not comfortable moving forward. And the reason they are not agreeing to move forward with the business opportunity most of the time is because they do not fully understand what the business and its requirements are all about and have not heard and responded to all the questions and research that was done.

Other details

Appointments will last about two hours. You will be asked to fill out and return a short Confidential Questionnaire prior to the appointment. As mentioned earlier, if you are married or will have business partners all parties should attend. And again, we don't charge for this process, but only meet with qualified candidates with a sincere desire to own their own business!

Random Q & A

Q: Should a franchise owner have a growth strategy in mind from the outset?

A: A business plan is as crucial for a franchise as it is for an independent business. Where do you want to go and what is the best way to get there? Will you make the money you wish with only one unit or territory? And how does the business fit with your personal goals? A person looking for a major career will have different objectives than a semi-retired person who wants to keep active and busy.

How To Properly Investigate Franchise Opportunities

Finding the right business is like finding the right job…only harder. Be prepared to spend lots of time doing your homework. If you do not feel you can afford the time, abandon your search now! A half-hearted attempt will prove to be a waste of your time and a waste of the franchise company's time. It's not too late to cancel your investigation before it gets involved, so make sure you are fully committed before proceeding. By the way, if you cannot or will not be in a position to return phone calls and/or keep appointments with franchisor representatives, this will reflect poorly on you. Please, either honor your commitments, or don't proceed.

Narrow the Field

The ultimate goal is for you to work through all the variables and narrow your choice down to one or two franchises and then make the final ultimate decision – do I move forward into business ownership or do I continue with what I am doing or doing something completely different.

However, be careful of the trap of eliminating a franchise too soon based on preconceived notions, insufficient investigation, etc. Sometimes a buyer will prejudge a franchise solely on the basis of sales literature about the franchise opportunity, or a first impression formed after a brief conversation with a franchisor representative. You may inadvertently eliminate the best one without realizing it! Be open to all possibilities and force yourself to review the literature, and have a follow-up conversation with the franchisor representative in order to fully understand their program and explore all of your concerns. To be even more open-minded, call one or two franchisees before you eliminate any of them. This will help to ensure that the end result and ultimate selection of a franchise is safe, affordable, and a great fit for you.

Work with your consultant

Take advantage of the help offered by your consultant/broker for the duration of your investigative or due diligence process. You do not compensate the consultant/broker; this is done by the franchisor if you buy a franchise. As your consultant, I seek the same thing you do—a proper selection of the right franchise opportunity for you. My business depends heavily on referrals from happy clients, so it will not grow if I am not helping you and meeting your needs. You should not hesitate to contact your consultant at any time with questions, concerns, comments, or just use them as a sounding board. I typically schedule follow-up meetings or telephone calls about 7-10 days apart. Each time, I review your progress thoroughly, answer more questions about individual programs, take stock of where the search is heading, and schedule a subsequent conversation.

The Investigation Process (Due Diligence)—General

Once you complete the initial consultation, the franchisor will have one of their representative(s) contact you. Typically, they will call to introduce themselves, follow up with a sales package, the Franchise Disclosure Document (FDD) if appropriate, and schedule an in-depth conversation. Please have this conversation with them in the time frame mutually agreed upon, or call them ahead of time to reschedule if you will have a conflict. Remember, these individuals are evaluating you on behalf of the franchise, just as you are evaluating their opportunity. Their time is as valuable to them as yours is to you.

Your next step may vary with the franchisor and their process. After an in-depth conversation with the franchise representative they may schedule telephone or in-person contact with franchisees. Alternately, you may be scheduled for a meeting with the franchise company itself, typically at their headquarters. This is called "Discovery Day". The purpose of Discovery Day is so they can get to know you better and go over in detail their system and get feedback from you. Other franchisors delay Discovery Day until you are further into the process and see a good fit for both franchisor and the potential buyer. Let the franchisor process evolve and make sense to you. Discovery Day is an important opportunity to get to know the people with whom you are considering going into business. Incidentally, some franchisors will help you with the expense of coming to Discovery Day, but this should not be a deciding factor in your decision to visit.

Final note on Discovery Day.

Do your homework before going! Don't go with the idea that the franchisor is going to put on a "dog-and-pony show" for you and that's it. You're there to learn everything that is important *to you*, not just what they want you to know. Have your questions ready, and make sure they get asked *and* answered.

The Business Model

In the course of investigating franchises, your attitudes about your needs and wants may change somewhat. The process itself is a learning experience. You may find that you started out looking at the wrong franchise(s), and need to change directions. At the writing of this guide, I have about 120 franchises I can work with. Don't waste time on companies you are truly not interested in. If your business model changes or the initial business you are reviewing don't seem quite right, with your feedback I can adjust the search accordingly.

The FDD

The FDD will play a big role in helping your investigation become as safe and accurate as possible. When you receive it, review it carefully. It's long and tedious, but full of great information that will assist and inform you. Your investigation tools will include a good highlighter, a red pen, a stack of post-it notes, your business plan (and maybe a few cups of coffee!).

Financing

Many franchise investments require some form of financing to capitalize the venture. You should look at various options to find the best one to fit your situation. This has been covered in other sections of this guide in Section Two under a topic called Finance options and Section Eight under topics called SBA Program and Other finance options. The franchise companies can offer suggestions for financing, and I have a number of sources I can recommend to you as well. If a franchisor has any type of internal financing source, they will disclose it in the FDD.

Personal Living Expenses

You should have funds or a funding source in place to cover personal living expenses for a six to twelve month period prior to starting your new venture. You don't want to rely on profits from the business too soon and you want to start your new venture with a conservative, reasonable and safe financial plan.

Final Decision

So, you've spent hours reading the franchise information and the FDD, you've spoken with representatives of the franchise, as well as franchisees, and even visited the franchise company's offices and/or franchisee's locations. You feel comfortable that you have found a safe, affordable, positive match for you. You're not done yet! You have one more thing to do. Go back to the beginning of your search when you formulated your Business Plan to look at the elements that you wanted in your franchise business. Does the one you think is right for you contain all those elements? Make sure the one you pick matches *your* business and personal goals and *your* specific business preferences. Don't settle!

Finally, ask questions, enjoy the process, as it's a big moment in your life.

List any questions you want to ask your consultant, advisor or franchisor.

End Of Chapter Notes

Use this page to write down notes, ideas and other brainstorming for buying your franchise.

Let's Get Started

"Do the difficult things while they are easy and do the great things while they are small. A journey of a thousand miles must begin with a single step."

Lao Tzu

Introduction

Sections one and two of this guide provides some background information about selling a business. Section three allows you to research and prepare your business for sale. The goal of sections four through eight is to provide a systematic approach to selling a business to enhance the chances of success at the best price. This is the model I use as a business broker and corresponds to the methods endorsed by the International Business Brokers Association and the California Association of Business Brokers—and I am a member of both of these organizations.

Assemble Your Team

The first step is to bring together the team you need to help you buy your franchise as quickly as possible. In section two we talked about the different professionals and their skills you can hire to help you. Now is the time to finalize the members of your team so you are ready to move forward.

To finalize the members of your team, go back to Section Two and start at page 48 to re-read this section. Your goal is to decide what professional help you need, if necessary, interview suitable professionals to ensure there is a match for you and the person you will be working with, negotiate any costs involved and move on.

Make your final selection on the basis that this will be a long term relationship. If a professional is not working for you there is no problem making a change; in fact it makes no sense other than to do that. The downside is that finding a replacement can take time and it may not be when you have downtime to do this but need that service now. It may mean you lose momentum or the opportunity you have been waiting for.

To find the professionals you need, the best place to start looking is with your immediate family and friends and people you trust. Your family and friends know you and what you're about and should be able to help and from their circle of influence suggest some people for you. If this doesn't address your need, there are some suggested places back in Section two.

In deciding who these people should be, take into consideration:
1. The skills they bring; you don't want someone with the same skill set if it clashes with your own.
2. The amount of time they have to help you and whether they will be readily available.
3. The costs involved in hiring the experts you need.
4. Whether you like it or not, one of the most important skills you will want from these people is emotional support and empathy in that they understand what you are going through and their advice is in your best interest and your best interest only. But most important of all, you want someone that will give you an honest answer to tough questions.

Use the following chart to write down the names of primary and secondary people you need for your team.

Service required	Option 1	Option 2	Option 3
CPA			
Attorney			
Personal Financial Planner			
Consultant/Business Broker	Andrew Rogerson ☺		

Once you build your team, try to avoid changing it.

Buying a business is a complicated process. If you surround yourself with good advisors and have a strong focus, you will get to the place of being able to make a decision that is right for you. If you have to change an advisor, then bad decisions can ensue as the new advisors may not be aware of all the nuances or you may miss a critical deadline.

First Contact With Your Business Broker Or Consultant

If you have been looking at buying a business you may have already built a relationship with your business broker. If you feel good about the relationship including the level of trust, set up a date and time to meet so you can understand the consulting process they use for someone who wants to buy a franchise. If I have been working with a buyer on previous transaction, I am comfortable having that meeting over the phone.

If this is the first contact you're having with the business broker or consultant, suggest a face-to-face meeting so both parties can get to know each other. If at all possible, I want both the buyer and their spouse/partner to attend all meetings. If this happens I can ensure all questions and concerns are being addressed and that both parties are on board with all the decisions being made and process to follow.

The main goal of the first meeting is so I can hand over the Buyer Qualification Profile, explain the importance of creating a business plan and provide an overview of the process we are going to follow. The other main goal is to also answer questions so what's being discussed makes sense for all the parties involved.

Completing The Questionnaire

The Buyer Qualification Profile is fairly straight forward so I am not going to go over it in great detail. I expect questions from the buyer and as each set of questions varies with each person I respond accordingly. The goal is to have the buyer complete and bring it to a mandatory face to face consultation which can last anywhere from 2 to 3 hours. We go over the document in detail but more importantly, ask a series of questions so we can drill down and find one or two franchise options that match the business plan and personal model the buyer has decided is important to them.

Face To Face Consultation

Once the Buyer Qualification Profile is returned, a face to face meeting is scheduled with the buyer and their spouse/partner. This meeting lasts anywhere from 2 to 3 hours and goes over a series of questions that require an answer so I can isolate one or two franchises that fit the business model we build during the consultation. There are many questions we cover in the consultation but here's a sample with it including items such as:
- Buyer goals – both professionally and personally.
- What venue does the buyer prefer to work from – Home/Office, Commercial office, retail etc.
- Are you willing to relocate for the right opportunity?
- Do you enjoy managing employees – if so, how many?
- Are the hours you work important to you, that is, are you OK with retail hours or do you prefer Monday through Friday only?
- Do you enjoy sales calls or prefer customers to come to you? Do you enjoy cold calling?

Towards the end of the consultation, once everything is making sense to the buyer, it's my goal to go over the next steps in the process and suggest one or two franchises for the buyer to research.

If the buyer agrees and would like to move forward and start researching a franchise, I will contact the franchise and introduce the buyer to them. My reason for doing this is so I can provide the buyer's background to the franchise including a copy of their resume and why we think this could be a good fit for the franchisor and the franchisee; knowing it's the buyers and franchisor's ultimate decision to decide if they want to work with each other. This contact includes providing the phone number and best time for the franchisor to call the buyer.

The buyer should then expect contact from the franchisor in the next day or two. Almost all the franchisors have their own process to follow. This varies according to the type of franchise and the processes they use with my preference to let the process evolve as it makes sense to both parties. It may be that the franchisor calls and introduces their contact person(s), explains the process they use and sends, generally by email, some preliminary information for the buyer to read including the Franchise Disclosure Document and schedule a second meeting. Sometimes the franchisor has a contact person call and goes over very basic introductions and sends through the material and schedules a second meeting once the buyer has a chance to review the material sent to them. Once the material arrives from the franchisor, move to the next section and continue with the process.

The 5-step Research Plan

Without question, the quality of research you undertake to make sure you buy the right franchise is paramount. What follows is a process to research a franchise so you can decide if this is the right option for you. This process has come from my personal experience as a five-time business owner and more importantly, as a business broker working in an industry that deals with buyers (and sellers) on a full time basis. It is a "strategic" process which means it is flexible and can be adapted but the thrust of this plan should work regardless of what you are looking to buy. However, feel free to adapt this plan to your needs and your style. Remember: only you can make the important final decision about buying your own franchise. As you work through your final decision you need solid information. Ultimately, how you obtain that information is a personal choice.

In summary, the five steps are:

1. Decide if you are going to use a Business Plan. It's my recommendation you do so as a good business plan template will ask questions I guarantee you will not have considered. Additionally, your business plan will evolve with your research. Having one central place to write down your research and questions that should spin from it for additional follow up is quickest, easiest and most efficient. If you use a business plan, keep it as a Work In Progress so you can adapt it based on new information as it's received.

2. Read the Franchise Disclosure Document and take notes about any questions you want the franchisor to answer. Highlight the sections you may wish your attorney to explain.

3. Glean "inside" information from the people who run the business on a daily basis by placing 8 to 10 telephone interviews with the franchisees. *There is no one better equipped to tell you what you need to know.* If approached properly, you will find the majority of the franchisees to be very forthcoming with useful answers. To make the most of your learning, *you will have to conduct telephone interviews and visit franchisees* in their places of business. This will take about six hours of work.

4. Visit the home office of the franchisor to obtain first-hand impressions of the franchisor's staff.

5. Use *experienced* professional advisers to help you – a *franchise* attorney and a good accountant.

Use the service and help of your consultant to answer ANY issue or item that concerns you. As I do this for a profession, to use a football analogy, I see my role as the coach on the side lines interpreting and offering clarity with your role as the Quarterback deciding how to execute the play but coming back to the coach if there is a need to clarify anything or call a time out so your team can re-group and decide if a different play is necessary. Use this workbook to collect your data and guide you on the appropriate processes to follow. Write the data in this workbook and transfer it to your business plan so you can make sure all questions are being addressed and no issue is being left behind.

Pace and Cost

This is a moderately paced but steady approach that will help you make a sound decision in two to three weeks. There is little or no expense for the first two steps. Also, make sure you challenge yourself to determine your level of interest at the end of each step.

Important:

Make these your two guiding research principles:

1. Value any opinion <u>only</u> by how informed it is.
2. Dig deep and learn from the experts - the franchisor and the franchisees. Remember: the franchisees serve as a "check" on any claim the franchisor can make.

Just as important:

Either commit to doing intelligent research, or do not start. Do not waste your time (and others' time) by "making a few calls" and pretending that is research. It is not! Remember: The true experts on the business are the franchisor and franchisees.

If you will not commit to that, you are probably not serious about the research - so don't start. This decision is too important for you to anything but intelligent, thorough and focused research.

Step One

1. If you've decided to use a Business Plan, start that process. Don't be too detailed in these early stages but keep it updated. The more you use this document the more you will come to rely on it and see how useful it is. If you arrive at a roadblock, record it in your business plan so it's not forgotten. That roadblock may then disappear as you get more information or decide that wasn't as much of a problem as you first thought. That's the beauty of a business plan. It keeps you focused and on target.

Step Two

1. Read the Franchise Disclosure Document.
    a. By law, about 90% of the FDD must be written in "plain English." Do not be intimidated by the FDD. This document may seem technical, so as you read, compile two lists of questions, one for the franchisor and the other for franchisees. Use the templates I have started in this work book to jump start this process. Highlight sections that you may wish your attorney to explain at a later date, if you do not receive satisfactory answers from the franchisor and franchisees.
    b. Interview franchisees. Commit to completing eight to ten telephone appointments with franchisees. View these as structured interviews, and you are the interviewer; and once again, use the questions I have started for you in this workbook.

Do not expect the franchisee to stop everything to talk to a stranger, and do not expect the franchisee to return calls to a stranger. Rather, introduce yourself, explain that you are researching the franchise, and ask when it will be convenient for you to call back. *Make a telephone appointment, at your cost but at the convenience of the franchisee.* Once you reach the franchisee, first establish rapport with the franchisee, asking them to "please help you out." Take complete notes of each interview and record your results in your business plan.

2. Write questions for the franchisor (use the list provided to start).
Interviews with franchisees will trigger questions for the franchisor. I have provided a preliminary set of questions but this will lead to more as you gather more information. Keep track of all questions in your business plan so as they are answered your business plan is updated. When you complete the first round of interviews with the franchisees and the business is still of interest to you, call the

franchisor to get answers to these new questions you've uncovered. *Again, keep that business plan current with your notes, observations and opinions.*

3. Check your level of interest.

Your first step is complete. Now ask yourself: "Am I still interested? Is my interest growing or declining?" If your interest is not strong, then stop. If you decide to continue your research, then move on to Step Three.

Step Three
1. Revise your questions.
Edit the list of questions in your business plan for the franchisees. If you received the same answer from eight to ten people, chances are you have learned all you can, so move on. Add to the list any new questions that came as a result of your previous interviews.

2. Interview more franchisees.
Plan to complete another eight to ten telephone interviews with franchisees. What you are doing is confirming what you heard on the first round. *Again, take careful notes*, and also compile a list of more questions for the franchisor.

3. Have more questions for the franchisor.
Call the franchisor with your new list of questions. *Take complete notes and update your business plan.*

4. Check your interest level again.

By this time, you have a very solid and basic understanding of the business from your 16+ interviews of franchisees. Still interested? Then move to Step Four.

Step Four
Up to this point, you have spent some time and some money on telephone calls but you have learned a great deal, and from reliable sources. Now you will incur some additional expense.

1. Arrange to visit franchisees.
Plan to complete three or more visits with franchisees in their places of business. *Prepare by making a list in your business plan of what you want to learn before you go*. The franchisees will know you are a serious person by the amount of research you have already completed. Thanks to that research, you are now ready to learn a great deal more.

Some of the unspoken questions *you are asking yourself* are: "*Can I see myself doing this business? Will I like it? Is it what I have been looking for?*"

Caution: Local franchisees may have mixed feelings about helping you. They may see you as a resource for growing the business *or* they may see you as a potential competitor for future locations!

2. Check your interest level. After completing the visits ask yourself: "Am I still interested?" If so, move on to Step Five.

Step Five

1. Visit the home office of the franchisor. By now, you have all the factual data you need, and should have your mind pretty much made up. Also have your contact person schedule appointments for you with key players: officers, managers of training, accounting, operations, and customer service. Treat these as formal interviews by planning your questions including what you want to learn. They will be sizing you up, but you should be sizing them up as well!

You want quality people as your senior partners in this business, not the bozos, so allow your intuition to answer this question: *"Are these the kind of people I want as my (senior) partners?"*

2. Once again, check your interest level.

After completing the visits ask yourself: "Am I still interested?" If so, go on to...

3. Obtain qualified professional advisers such as a franchise attorney and a good small business accountant. But only do this if your research is going well. Also, do this prior to going to the home office so you can decide if there are outstanding legal questions you would like addressed by the franchisor.

Caution #1: Hire an attorney for his *legal advice,* not his business opinion. Sometimes attorneys will offer uninformed opinions about the franchise! The truth is, if you have followed this system and performed good research, you know more about the business - not the law - than the attorney does. When you hire your attorney, a good starting point is to ask what they would charge to review the FDD plus any additional help you need including creating your legal entity.

Also, hire a qualified accountant to review the financial strength of the franchisor, and advise you of the economics of the opportunity, plus give you guidance on financing.

Caution #2: Once again, hire an accountant for their *accounting skill,* not their business opinion. Sometimes accountants also offer uninformed opinions about the franchise!

Remember the four critical questions:
1. What does the successful owner do? (You know this through your research.)
2. Can I do or learn to do what the successful owner does? (You know what your own skills and knowledge are.)
3. Do I want to do what the successful owner does? (Trust your intuition here!)
4. If I do what the successful owner does, will I get what I want? (Check it against your model's goals that came from your consultation.)

Conclusion

Now you have a mountain of information and impressions about the franchise. You also have the advice of professionals such as a franchise attorney and an accountant. You are prepared to decide: *"Is this for me?"* Whether the answer is yes or no, *you can be confident that you carried out an intelligent and diligent investigation.*

If you follow each of the Five Steps, you will have all the answers you need to make the final intelligent decision. Always remember that YOU are the one making the investment and the life choice. *The best decision is the one that will work for you.* No matter what that decision turns out to be, if you have done your research properly, you will significantly improve your likelihood of making the best decision.

Receive, Read And Review The FDD

Once you receive the FDD from the franchisor it's time to sit down in a quiet place and go over its content. If you want to refresh yourself on the content of what's in the FDD, go back to Section two and re-read the topic about the FDD and other transaction documents on page 38. You can go over this section on your own, with your spouse/partner/friend, with your attorney or with your consultant. My suggestion is that you read it at least three times. Read it quickly the first time so you get a feel for the document and then put it down. Read it slower and with more attention to detail and write down questions about topics as you go. Use the "box" below to write down questions and again put it aside. Now get all your questions answered and when you have another quiet moment, read the FDD in full once again and write down any questions you may now have. If you feel comfortable about all the details, move on.

The other important task to do as you work through the FDD is to keep updating your business plan. Understanding the FDD and simultaneously working on your business plan will keep you focused and heading in the right direction.

Write down questions you want to research further as you read the FDD.

First Main Contact With Your Franchisor

To help facilitate the process, the next section below has two sets of documents for the buyer to use. The first set of documents covers what I call fact questions. That is, the questions pretty much have definite answers and are not subject to an opinion. From my perspective, the fact questions provide the foundation for moving forward. If the buyer is uncomfortable with the data in the fact questions, they probably don't need to move forward with this franchise but start looking for another. It's also helpful to move this data into the Business Plan as it should stimulate questions and/or additional research.

My suggestion is to use the fact questions below as a starting point by either adding these to your business plan with additional questions you think of that are relevant to your type of franchise. Alternatively, you can add additional questions to the supplemental notes at the end of the fact questions.

The second set of questions is a suggested list of opinion questions to ask the franchisor. Once again, add your own questions and bring them together with their answers in your business plan so you can keep everything in one place. By following this process of questions, research, more questions and more research, consultations will get you to where you need to be.

Random Q & A

Q: What are some common misconceptions about franchise ownership?

A: The biggest mistake is to believe that franchises never fail. Although the failure rate is much lower than that of independent business, the franchisee still must have the necessary commitment and drive. Also, franchise owners have no special legal protection after they purchase the business. The Franchise Disclosure Document (FDD), a legal document that lays out the rules and requirements for full disclosure, only protects the buyer before the sale. Finally, a common misconception deals with the goals of the franchisor and franchisee. The one common thread between the two is building the brand. Other than building the brand, the franchisor and franchisee may not have congruent goals.

Fact Questions For The Franchisor

The table below provides a prompt to help you get going with your process of buying your franchise. Use the table below to ask these fact questions and at the bottom of this table, add any other questions that are important to you. **Remember: There is no such thing as a stupid question.**

Date _____   Time _____

Write Franchisor's URL: If applicable: Username: Password: Any other links to presentations, marketing materials and articles here:	

Company History ❖ President and Founder(s) ❖ Vision and goals ❖ Date founded and began franchising ❖ Number of locations (franchised and company owned) and regions sold ❖ Projected new locations within next year ❖ Registration state issues ❖ Marketing plan	
Company Description ❖ Industry focus ❖ Type of services/goods ❖ Location type required ❖ Location size and variables ❖ General operating hours ❖ Staff requirements ❖ Average price per sale ❖ Target market ❖ Sale average per location ❖ Required systems/equipment ❖ Competitive edge provided	

Advantages Offered	
❖ Training type(s)/length ❖ Advertising type(s) ❖ Financing assistance ❖ Location/site selection assistance ❖ Lease negotiation assistance	
Anticipated Returns	
❖ Estimated average net ❖ Estimated average break-even point ❖ Estimated profit margin ❖ Financial analysis of existing location ❖ Anchoring (locations with highest volumes)	
Terms of Investment	
❖ Investment range ❖ Required minimum net worth ❖ Fees (franchise, royalty, advertising) ❖ Splits (franchise fee/royalty)	
FAQs	
❖ What makes this company unique? ❖ How do you capture your target consumer? ❖ What unique features attract franchisees? ❖ Will you consider launch of a location without a regional developer in place?	

Supplementary notes and additional questions.

Questions To Ask Franchisors On The First Call

Here are some more questions to ask the franchisor. These questions are more open and subject to an opinion so don't be afraid to ask the same question in a different manner to make sure you get an answer that makes sense to you. And as always, please add your own questions. This is what this guide is all about plus it will reflect well on you with your Franchisor by showing you are thinking deeply about what you are doing.

Question	Answer/Comment
Competitive Advantage	
What makes the business attractive to me as an owner and why?	
What makes the business attractive to a customer and why?	
How is their system better than their competitors and why?	
Who are your competitors and why?	
Standardized franchise system	
Ask for a description of how their franchise system works and what improvements they have made recently.	
How long have they been franchising?	
How many franchise units do they have?	
How many units have they closed in the last three years? Why?	
How many units have been transferred or sold in the last three years? Why?	
How many units have they opened in the last three years?	
How many units do they plan to open in the next three years?	

Question	Answer/Comment
What is the function of the business?	
What is the function of the owner?	
What does the owner have to do to be successful?	
What is the initial investment? And what does it include.	
Describe their fees.	
Ask if they have an earnings claim in their Franchise Disclosure Document? If so, what is it?	

Franchisor support	
Describe the support: initial and on-going training, 800-help-lines, field support, annual meetings, local meetings, purchasing, marketing, etc.	
What support do they provide franchisees?	
Describe the initial training.	
What support is available after the business is open?	
What will you hear from the franchisees on this subject?	

Franchisor financial and management strength	
Describe the financial and management experience of the franchisor. (The comments will help you to understand the FDD after you get the document.)	

Mutual interests
(These questions you can ask both the franchisor and the franchisees.)

How will the franchisees describe their relationship with the franchisor?	
Is it supportive? Is it combative?	
Have there been any lawsuits or arbitration?	
What were the issues, and how did it end?	

Your Questions

End Of Chapter Notes

Use this page to write down notes, ideas and other brainstorming for buying your franchise.

Validations

> *"For true success ask yourself the following four questions:*
> *Why? Why not? Why not me? Why not me now?"*
>
> *James Allen*

Introduction

This phase of buying your franchise involves you doing most of the work to research the suitability of buying your franchise. Specifically it involves doing three main things so you can arrive at the next critical decision: whether or not buying the franchise is making sense to you, and then whether you want to attend the franchisors Discovery Day. These are:

1. Continue working with your business plan to build the answers to all the questions you've thought about (and the many more questions you will uncover).
2. Talk with franchisees and other qualified parties to assess their success and whether or not the ownership of this franchise is right for you.
3. Bring this altogether to see if you want to invest further by attending the franchisors Discovery Day.

Validations

These next steps of your process are some of the most important as you will interview the current franchise operators to get their view of working with the franchisor. To ensure the integrity of your research, as you contact the franchisees it is critical to ask the same questions of all the franchisees to:

1. See how well the concept fits your business plan.
2. Understand what degree the franchise concept meets your financial goals.
3. See how well the franchisor supports its franchisees.
4. See if you feel comfortable in the role of the franchisee.
5. Who demonstrates similar traits to you – top performers or underperformers?

Contacting the franchisees

In the next section, we have a list of questions to ask the franchisee who currently owns and operates the franchise (one of the most important sources of information for you. Franchisees can provide a wealth of information (and opinions) about the franchise company, the industry, and how to be either successful or unsuccessful. Call or visit a minimum of 6-10 of them as part of your due diligence.

Here are a few guidelines to help you get the most out of your contact with franchisees:

✓ Don't *expect* them to return calls to you. You aren't putting any money in their pockets. They're doing you a favor (although they probably asked others to do them the same favor when they were investigating the franchise). Respect their time; ask them to identify a good time to spend a few minutes with you, and make the phone call at your cost.

✓ In order to get the most comprehensive and honest answers from existing franchisees, assure them at the beginning of the call that anything they say will be kept in the strictest of confidence.

✓ Be prepared. Have your questions ready at the beginning of the conversation, know where you are heading, and don't let the call take more than an agreed amount of time.

✓ When you are asking about the financial performance of the business, be sensitive with how you ask your question. After warming up the conversation for a few minutes, ask them if they had any income expectations when they went into the franchise, what were those expectations, and then ask them if those expectations have been met. Or, ask them in general terms about the income opportunity of their franchise company. If you create a *relationship* before you start asking financial questions you will have much greater success getting a quality answer.

✓ Most franchisees want the system to grow, just not in their own backyard. Be sensitive to the local franchisees that know that you are looking to buy in their general area. There's plenty of business to go around, or the franchise company would not be offering another franchise in the area. However, not all existing franchisees welcome another "competitor" and discourage growth as they think it could cost them business, or they want to take advantage of growth in that area themselves.

✓ Most franchise prospects call franchisees at random, hoping to find the ones that are not doing well, as if that were the way to ferret out "the truth". This approach will not take you where you want to go! Talk to 5-7 franchisees that are doing well, *and ask them what it takes to be successful with that franchise.* If you bring to the table those required attributes, and a desire to do the things you must do to be successful, then maybe this is the perfect franchise for you. As to those who are not doing well, consider that they may be a fish out of water. Remember, compare yourself to the franchisees who are doing well. If you feel you are like them, you may have a winner! If you feel you are more similar to the ones who are struggling, walk away.

✓ Some franchisees just don't want to spend time with you discussing the franchise. This is not a reflection on the franchise (or you!). Some people are just not as helpful as others and don't want to take the time to have a conversation that does not directly improve their income. Move on to another franchisee, and disregard the contact.

✓ Don't overinvest in comments from one specific franchisee be it exceptionally good or bad. Your goal is to get a variety of opinions and ultimately decide if this franchise would be a good match for you with the skills and personality that you bring.

✓ Finally, try to ask the same set of questions to each franchisee that you speak. Your goal is to have the same set of data so if you ask each franchise a different set of questions you don't have a quality set of data to determine if this is the right option for you. This is the process used by polling companies; for their data to be reliable they have to ask the same question in a consistent manner.

Your Questions For The Franchisees

Earlier in this chapter we interviewed the franchisor with a list of questions to see if their business model and its package made sense to us. Now it's time to interview some of the franchisees. Their contact details are in the Franchise Disclosure Document. Below are some suggested questions. Make sure you add your own. Additionally, after you talk to the first two franchisees think back on your questions and answers in case you want to modify any of these as well add your own. And here's a suggestion: ask each franchisee the same set of questions. Don't ask a different set of questions to each franchisee as that's poor research.

Are you happy with your relationship with the franchisor?
Do you enjoy doing what you do day-to-day?
Can you give me an idea of your typical day?
Have you been satisfied with your economic results?
Have the bottom-line economics of the business generally met or exceeded your expectations?
Would you recommend this business to a close relative or a good friend?
Would you like to have a second unit?

If you had to do it over, would you buy the franchise again?
Has the franchisor delivered what they promised and been there for you when you've needed them? Are the people that run the franchise honest and fair?
Is the franchisor a straight shooter and do they keep their word?
Are you better off being part of this system than trying to start in the business as an independent?
Do you have any other information or advice that you feel would be helpful for someone looking to get into your business?
Are you making as much money from this franchise as you expected you would make?
What are the primary challenges facing your franchise organization and what is the franchisor doing to address them?

Competitors

When planning to purchase a new TV or major appliance, you check out prices and deals to make sure you have the best price and service. Now that you are planning to buy your franchise, it makes sense to do the same with your top three competitors for the following reasons:

1. To see how your franchise would compare with things like location, customer service, employee attitudes, customer attitudes etc.
2. To check prices to make sure you would be competitive.
3. To check the appearance of their business compared to yours in case you will need to "out compete" them by putting in a better quality business; if this is important to the business.

Make a list of questions below and then without identifying yourself, contact each of your three main competitors.

> **Write down questions to ask your competitors so you are better prepared when talking to a potential buyer.**

Random Q & A

Q: What else is essential to successful franchise ownership?

A: As with any other type of enterprise, you need to be genuinely interested in the type of business you're considering. If you want to buy a tax preparation franchise, for example, it is best to have excellent math skills and a long attention span. Remember that you will be living the business 24/7. You need to be certain that you can accept some level of sacrifice in your personal life, and that your family will support this kind of commitment.

Updating Your Business Plan

This is a reminder to keep your business plan up-to-date and current. You should be continually researching and asking many questions. This leads to learning and absorbing a whole lot of information. And because you are learning you need to write things down as it should create questions and the need to do further research. And here's a great benefit I've found. Once I write it down I can forget about it and deal with it at the appropriate time.

Discovery Day

If you are moving through your research and it's making sense for you to continue with your interest in buying a specific franchise, your next major decision point will be deciding if you want to attend a Discovery Day organized by that franchisor.

Discovery Day is essentially a visit to the franchisor's home or corporate office. You get to meet not only the people you have been working with remotely but also to see first-hand the corporate operation. Also, in a lot of cases, the franchisor has a working franchise you are able to visit to see how things are done or they will arrange for you to visit a working franchise so you see firsthand the operation and what their franchise is all about.

To attend a Discovery Day you will need to be invited by the franchisor and they will explain the cost to attend the event. In most cases, you will be responsible for the air-fare, hotel costs and meals with the franchisor then providing the transport and meeting venue to demonstrate their product or service. Once again, this is the time to make lots of notes and answer more questions.

The process is not the same for each franchisor, but attending a Discovery Day suggests the franchise is of great interest to you and that you are moving towards a final decision. Section Six is where we bring it all together so you can make that final decision about this particular franchise.

Serious Advice For Serious Buyers

If you've read this guide right through to this point you will hopefully agree this guide is not trying to sell you anything. In fact, my approach is the reverse where I need you as the franchise buyer to do the work and then decide if buying a franchise is right for you. My hope is that if there is a business that will give you what you want, is it worth looking for? Most people will answer "yes" to that question. So, why do so few who say they want business ownership finally end up owning a business? There are many reasons, of course. One important reason is that many potential franchise buyers simply lose their focus during the research period. They blame it on external reasons, and then just drift away from their dream. If you see yourself as a serious looker for a franchise business, consider the following.

1. Have a research plan and set a deadline.

Successful business owners including franchisees are invariably goal oriented. Copy them by setting a realistic date for completing your research process. Break your plan down into shorter goals so you feel like you are making progress. If you hit a roadblock, clearly define the problem, determine your options and choose the option that makes the most sense and keep moving forward. For example, on your plan, determine that you will complete Step one in seven days, Step two in three days etc. Do not pressure yourself, but maintain a steady pace.

Let the franchisors and your consultant know your target dates. That will focus them to complete their information gathering process about you on the same schedule. Also, they will respect your goal setting and follow-through abilities. Be organized. Be serious. Set a schedule, and stick to it.

2. Protect your reputation.

Buying a franchise is not like buying a car. While you are evaluating the franchise, the franchisor is evaluating you. Cars do not do that (at the moment)! A quality franchisor does not "sell" franchises in a transactional manner. Rather, they want to sign a long term contract with someone who will be a high performer in their system. For both the franchisor and the franchisee this is not a short term investment. They want someone who knows themselves and asks good questions. They want someone who is responsible so do what you say you will do. They want someone they can work with, so be assertive, but be cooperative. You want to make yourself desirable to a quality franchise system. It is in your interest to protect your reputation! Be the quality prospect that quality franchisors desire.

3. Don't settle until it ALL makes sense…or move on.

While you are the only one who can do the research and make the decision, you can have advisers to help you. This includes an attorney, an accountant, and people like me. Like the franchisor I mentioned above, my job is NOT to sell you anything. If you feel you this is the sole purpose of the person you work with then find someone else. My sole goal is to help you find what you want. If I do that successfully then I am paid. I am there as your coach and consultant. I am as near as your telephone, and willing to visit with you again, if you wish. In fact, I will call you frequently to ask how your research and due diligence is going towards getting to your goal and how I can help. If a franchise will not lead you to your goals, what is missing from the franchise so we can learn from this and move on? Or…do you now want to change your goals or your model?

It is perfectly OK to change your goals or your model or both! It is the number one reason for doing the research. You learn about the franchises, about what is available, and you learn about yourself. If you want to make a change, that is great! It means you are clarifying your ideas, getting a sharper focus...and going after what you really want. You tell me what you have changed, and then I can help you find a better fit. So, do not settle. Get what you want!

4. You will get nervous

Buying a business is a serious decision. No one makes a serious decision without getting a little nervous. Having bought and sold five businesses and looked at many more, the nervousness helps tell me where I am at. If I don't get nervous it may mean this is not the best option for me and my family.

Can you make a good decision even if you do get nervous? You have done it many times in your life already. Good, solid, serious research and good advisers will lead you to a good decision. Do not over-look this part of the process. It's perfectly human and perfectly normal. If you are still unsure, include this as a question to ask the franchisees you speak with. They made good decisions and possibly without all the solid research and reliable advice available to you. Certainly, they were nervous at some point, probably several points.

If you have gathered the right information, and are honest about your own abilities, you will make a smart, educated decision for yourself....despite the butterflies! Expect to get nervous. Deal with it. Don't let nerves steal your dream.

Random Q & A

Q: What is your best bit of practical advice to prospective franchise owners?

A: Spend time up front doing the research. There is no hurry. Once the franchise is yours, you own it. Make sure it fits into your lifestyle—and that it is something you will enjoy doing—and it will make the money your business plan projects.

End Of Chapter Notes

Use this page to write down notes, ideas and other brainstorming for buying your franchise.

Section Six

Review your options

Introduction

It's only time to move to this section – review your options – if you have done the work in your business plan, made the calls, talked to your key advisors and want to arrive at a final decision. Your final decision may include many options. These include:

1. Going back to the Franchisor you've been working with and asking more questions.
2. Deciding one particular franchise is not a good fit and that you'd like to investigate another franchise.
3. Deciding that business ownership is not right for you at the moment.

Before you make a final decision I would recommend that you bring all your research together and discuss it in detail with your business broker or consultant. If the matter is crystal clear in your mind, then by all means move forward with your purchase. However, if there are outstanding questions (and there should be) now is the time to get them on the table and addressed.

Review Your Options

These next three topics are designed to provide you with a snapshot of where you are and highlight any areas you'd like to work on to improve your final decisions and be fully prepared for the next steps of buying your franchise. The first piece is a quick and dirty SWOT analysis. A SWOT analysis looks at Strengths, Weaknesses, Opportunities and Threats.

The second topic is to update or refresh your business plan. The third and final topic is something I call a Reality Check. Its purpose is to provide a moment to pause, look at all the data you've collected and analyzed so far, and make the final decision that buying your franchise is really what you want to do.

SWOT analysis

A SWOT analysis helps you identify strengths, weaknesses, opportunities or threats. In this case, we are doing the SWOT analysis to decide if buying a franchise is the right option for you or there are outstanding issues to resolve.

Strengths will give you confidence this is the right direction to go while weaknesses and threats will be red flags that may indicate the need for more research. Opportunities can go either way but should mean that the item is not that critical and you're comfortable with the outcome either way.

Use some of the prompts below and place them in one of the boxes— strength, weakness, opportunity or threat. Make sure you add your own items that are important to you as you want to consider all the variables.

Once you've completed the exercise, consider discussing the weaknesses or threats. Again, make sure you brainstorm other "talking points" and place them in one of the boxes so you can do a final review and take any further action you deem necessary. Go back to the original Buyer Qualification Profile to see if that triggers any talking points.

Considerations for Your SWOT Analysis

✓ State of the national but more importantly, the local economy
✓ Industry - growing or contracting?
✓ Interest rates - declining or increasing?
✓ Is yours an interest rate-sensitive business?
✓ Lease – can you get one in line with market rate and with renewal options?
✓ Business style – have you found the opportunity that meets your criteria?
✓ Does the business require trained management if the owner leaves? Is this part of your business model preference?
✓ Employees - regular training program in place?
✓ Operations manual - does the business have one?
✓ Customer base – easy to increase?
✓ Inventory level – easy to manage?
✓ Appearance of the business – is this important to you? Is it acceptable to you?
✓ Location of business?
✓ Good or bad public image of the industry and is this important to you?

Strength	Weakness
Opportunity	**Threat**

Refresh Your Business Plan

You've spent a considerable amount of time and energy (and probably a few costs along the way) so it's time to bring your business plan up to date and see what's outstanding.

In no particular order I would suggest that you find a quiet place, and on your own, update your business plan with as many details as you can. The ultimate goal would be to have an answer for every item on your business plan so you can see what's outstanding. In order to do that, use the following process:

1. Open your business plan.
2. Update as many areas as you can.
3. Think of any new items you need to add since you last reviewed your business plan.
4. Answer as many of these as you can.
5. Go back over your business plan to decide the importance of each of the outstanding items by assigning a 1, 2 or 3. One means it's critical and you must have an answer before you move forward. Two means it's important but it's not a roadblock. Three means it's important but it will either solve itself as you move through the process or you're not going to worry about it.
6. Now take a break.
7. Come back to your business plan and revisit just the ones and twos. Decide how you want to address the ones. Do you talk to some more franchisees to get their opinion? Do you talk to the franchisor? Do you talk to your consultant or professional advisor? Or do you need to talk to a combination of these?
8. Now take a break.
9. Come back and review the two's by either moving them into a one and taking action or cross them off and letting them go. The idea is to let go of the two's that now don't have the importance they had when you first thought of them.
10. The bottom line is that you now want to start bring your research and hard work together so you can move to the next section below, which is doing a reality check and making a final decision. With a final decision comes action – which is what everything is about. As I've noted in the quote at the start of this section by Pablo Picasso – "Action is the foundational key to all success."

Reality Check

Now is your opportunity to sit back and look through the previous sections and weigh your final decision. You can review your notes, re-read your business plan and go back and reflect on your research.

The next step is then to make your final decision and best course of action and get on with it.

The table below suggests some options with additional space for you to add other options/ideas. Put a score of 1 to 10 in the right hand column next to each option. The more you like the idea, the higher the score. After you assign all scores, discard the lower scores and focus on the higher scores to make your final decision on your next steps...and then take action.

Option	Score
Do nothing – continue with whatever you have currently been doing	
Look for a business to buy	
Look for another franchise to buy	
Take a break and come back to this idea sometime in the future	

Random Q & A

Q: What are some musts to consider in evaluating franchise opportunities?

A: Prospective franchise owners should conduct the same thorough research that any new business owner should do. Franchisors cannot research each individual market, so it is the responsibility of the prospective franchisee to do his or her homework. The Internet is a wonderful source of information, but it's also helpful to literally "walk the street" and ask people if this kind of business is needed in the neighborhood. You should also study the competition. Find out what they are doing, and figure out how you can do it better. After all, you will have to do it better to succeed.

Top 11 Things To Do When Buying Your Franchise

Here's a list of 11 suggestions I've come across when consulting with business owners from all walks of life who were deciding whether to buy their first or eleventh business. Take advantage of some of the experiences I've come across and save yourself from some potential problems!

1. Buy a business that you can afford.

The two biggest dream killers of business ownership are under-capitalization and lack of experience. We all learn from our mistakes however this is the point of this guide and the process I am suggesting; if your goal is to attain business ownership through a franchise, speak to those who are successful so you can apply what you've learnt to your situation and make sure you buy a business you can afford.

2. Stay within your financial resources.

Never buy a business that you can't afford as it is the number one reason that businesses fail. They simply run out of cash to operate and advertise before they have enough customers and cash flow to support the business.

3. Only start looking for a business when you have an idea of what you want.

If you need to drive to a destination you have been to before you can use your previous knowledge to get part of the way, but it's the map that actually gets you to your destination…or your spouse/partner or GPS. Bottom line is that you need help and you need help in a logical order so you get to your destination. Many people look at owning a business without first determining what they are looking for. Some assume that all good businesses are good for all buyers. That's not the way it works. Would you buy the best restaurant in town if your background was working in the auto industry? Your skills, goals, values, and ambitions will all play a role in determining the best business for you. By using a little self-analysis and the consultation process, you will have a greater likelihood of successfully finding the right business for you.

4. Business ownership is hard work. If you're not up for it – don't start.

You may get lucky and find that bar and grill with slot machines that you buy will make your fortune with seemingly no effort, but that kind of success is relatively rare. You should plan on exactly the opposite for the franchise or business you start. Assume you will have to work longer and harder than others currently in the same business just to make it work. If you're not willing to do that then I suspect business ownership is not for you. When you're planning, be conservative. If there are going to be surprises, let them be pleasant ones. If you know in your heart that you can do what it takes to make a business succeed no matter how challenging it is, then you are well on your way towards success. If you're basing your chances for success on being among the operators who were pleasantly surprised by the effortless success of their businesses, you will often have exactly the opposite result.

5. Assemble a team and don't try to go it alone. Use experts.

Lack of experience is often cited as one of the two biggest killers of start up businesses. Certainly your franchisor will help you by sharing their experience with you, but use the experience of other experts as well. This is the reason in Section Four that I have you assemble your team. Sometimes we don't seek expert advice because we simply don't want to hear anything that does not agree with our hopes. That's a big mistake. If something is really wrong, it's better to find out before you're already deeply invested both financially and emotionally. Conversely, if something is wrong, it may be easy to fix if found early. Be sure to consult with financial experts, franchise consultants, and perhaps most importantly, a franchise attorney. We know that you like to avoid spending money that you feel you can save, but having an attorney who is knowledgeable about franchising review your offering before you buy could be a lifesaver. This is no different to the life insurance and auto insurance you probably have in place.

6. *Create and use a business plan.*

There are too many analogies to suggest the opposite. We wear warm clothes in winter, we put our money in the bank rather than under the bed to keep it safe, we take out different types of insurances, when we travel overseas we put together a plan for driving to the airport, flying to the nearest city and getting transport to a hotel and the start of our sightseeing. Before you invest into a business, in addition to investigating the franchise you are buying, also study both the local market in which you'll be operating and the industry that you are contemplating joining. The franchisor, and also other franchisees, can often tell you a lot about the national and local market and the trends in the industry, but don't stop there. Talk to the Chamber of Commerce, check out the internet, and do research through the industry reference books at the library. Investigate thoroughly and at the same time build your business plan. Get opinions of the experts around you and if you are not impressed, don't do it!

7. *Choose the franchise that makes sense to you – not because "there are so many of them, they must be good."*

When buying a business, feeling safe is a strong and undeniable urge. When you look at an already popular franchise, your safety level instinctively is high. Even though it's not a franchise, just think Starbucks. It looks pretty easy to operate and they are everywhere so how can you fail. Right?

Not necessarily! Sometimes too many good things can mean that competition is so fierce that the market is saturated and that there is little or no room for new operators. Additionally, just because you know how to do something doesn't mean you'll LIKE it! If you have a basic need for variety or for constant challenge, you may find that repetitive tasks, which are required in many businesses, would actually bore you to tears. Also, be sure to remember that the number of franchises in an area is no automatic indication of their financial potential. Some of the best franchises only allow one or two franchisees in an entire city, while others have dozens in a single marketplace.

8. *Make sure you talk with the other franchisees.*

Current business owners who are in a business that you find attractive are the best source of information that you'll ever find. But watch out – sometimes there may be a hidden agenda. If you wander into a dry cleaner, tell him you are thinking of going into dry cleaning, and ask his opinion, what value are you going to put on the response? Do you think he will give you an honest answer if he thinks you may be planning on opening a competitive outlet just down the street?

On the other hand, when you have done your homework with a franchisor, have read the FDD, and are calling franchisees all over the United States, you'll get valuable information that you can check out with others to see if it rings true throughout the franchise system.

It's important to find the people who are doing well in a franchise as well as to find people who are struggling. Which one are you most like? Do your skills match the winner? Or are there tasks that must be done in the business that you are unwilling or unable to do? If you hate cold calls and the business requires talking with every merchant in your territory, find something else. If your goal is to find a business that you will enjoy, then get the real facts from the people in the know: the franchisees.

9. *Make sure you have cash for the downpayment.*

Sure, you can put it on your credit card. But wow, those interest rates hurt. At 20% plus, you'd better hope that the cash flow starts very quickly! Chances are very strong that it won't. Most reputable franchisors would strongly discourage you from using this kind of financing if they feel it could impact your ability to succeed. Reputable franchisors not only want you to succeed but they *need* you to succeed – that's how they make their money. A franchisor charges a royalty, which is a percentage of your gross sales. In return, they give you service and support. If you don't make money, they don't make money, and they still are obligated to serve you. So if they don't think you can make it, they have many reasons to be frank with you.

10. Pick the franchise YOU like the most – not your dad (or sister.)

We are all unique with different skills, needs, and desires. Why would your dad or your neighbor or brother like the same businesses that you do? When you look at a business, you need to think about how it matches with the things that you truly want to do and whether it will fulfill your goals.

You need to analyze what is important to you. Things such as independence, money, freedom, flexibility, children, growth, challenge, variety, teaching, people? Each business can fulfill different types of needs. If you want freedom and flexibility of hours, then food and some other types of retail may be too demanding of your time – perhaps a service business where you can book your own appointments would be better for you. On the other hand, if you want high visibility, then perhaps retail would be perfect.

11. Love being in business – not the product.

If you like new motorcycles or coffee or candles or hand lotion or sporting gear or pizza or filling out tax returns – be careful. When you enjoy a certain type of product or service, it's natural to want to be around it. But retail is retail, so make sure you can do the things needed to make the business successful; that is running a business. It takes a certain personality type to do the things that retail demands such as manning the store hour after hour, day after day, being nice to your customers, making change, and keeping track of the inventory. It takes someone who loves schmoozing with everyone and being of service to others. It takes a team-builder to keep good employees.

Sure, you love those motorcycles and their accessories! But in the end, what you are doing with them is not putting them on your classic motorcycle – you're standing behind a counter selling them, putting them onto shelves, dusting them, and inventorying them.

When you pick a business, check out what you would be doing all day every day. Your dream, of course, will be to have other people pour the frozen smoothies or ring up the oil filters, but most young businesses will demand that you work there for at least the first few months to get the cash flow going and effectively train employees.

Many of us dream of being our own boss someday, and we know that it's impossible to take all the risk out of going into business for ourselves. Avoiding as many dumb mistakes as possible can certainly help us move the odds into our favor.

So, if we are to have our dreams fulfilled, we should approach the opportunity of owning our own business with our eyes open, and with the strength of knowledge and planning -- this is the formula for becoming a successful business owner!

Franchising Myth – The More You Spend

Sometimes what we hear if it's said over and over again becomes accepted as a fact, whether or not it is true. And so what develops is a myth, that is, a flawed or false belief. When it comes to franchising, there are a few myths that can be misleading or even destructive! In my experience, one myth stands out above all the rest as having the ability to be most misleading.

Myths often have their roots planted in something that would otherwise make sense. That's a big part of what makes them so believable. The myth that I have been alluding to certainly has such roots. When you are thinking of joining a franchised organization, you can gain a significant advantage if you can avoid the myths and deal only with facts. By recognizing what truly differentiates the facts from the fallacies, you can help yourself make a better and more productive decision. The most important myth that prospective franchise investors have is one that deals with how much it costs to acquire a franchise that can produce a lot of income for the franchisee. I call it: "The more money I invest in a business, the more money I will make "myth."

Many people incorrectly believe that the more they spend to buy a franchise, the better that franchise is going to be. It's easy to see why people might think this way, since in most areas of our lives, there is an understandable correlation between how much something costs, and how much benefit we derive from that purchase. In most of our minds, the more we spend, the more we expect to get. After all, why would anyone spend more money for something, unless they expected to get more for their money?

Ask yourself a simple question. If you were to see two houses in the same neighborhood, and one was selling for $100,000 and the other was selling for $200,000, wouldn't you expect the $200,000 house to be much nicer than the $100,000 home?

This same bit of logic makes sense in almost every area of our life. Nice cars cost more than cars that aren't as nice. Better sounding stereos cost more than those that don't produce sound of equal quality. Even the seats at a theater or sports arena are priced by the quality of the view that one gets. We all know it's true. When we pay more, we expect we will get more.

Be that as it may, when it comes to acquiring and opening a new franchised location it's just simply not automatically true. Am I saying that in franchising, it's possible to spend less, and get a business that has the potential to earn as much or more as a franchise that costs a lot more? The answer is absolutely YES! Can you believe it? It's counter-intuitive to believe that it's possible for one to spend less, yet get more. Despite this fact, when it comes to acquiring a new location for a franchise, it is unassailably true.

Interestingly enough, when it comes time to sell and exit a business, normal logic once again prevails. The more profitable a business, the more it usually can be sold for. But, in this one instance, when a business is first started, it remains true that the logic that says that the more we spend the more we should automatically get is suspended!

Think about it: do all good businesses cost the same amount to establish? Does a restaurant that is located in a retail shopping area cost the same amount to open as a consulting business that can be located in an office building, or even in a house? Of course not! A relatively modest restaurant can easily cost $300,000-500,000 to launch. There are extensive tenant improvements needed, as well as a lot of equipment, furnishings, and inventory. In fact, many restaurants can cost $750,000- $1,000,000 or more to open. However, despite the $1,000,000 or more needed to open some restaurants, there is absolutely no guarantee that once that restaurant opens its doors for business, that anyone will choose to eat there. And if they do, they may never come back! The only thing that can be said with certainty is that it will cost the owner $1,000,000 to find out!

In contrast, let's think about consultants. Have you ever met a consultant who owns his/her own company, makes a lot of money, and has a great business? Many of us have. Now ask yourself this: How much did it cost that consultant to start their business? Usually, not very much. A restaurant's customers come to the restaurant to eat. With a consultant, it's usually the other way around. Consultants go to their client's place of business so the consultant will not need to spend a lot of money to build the "physical plant" that a restaurant would require. As such, consulting businesses do not need as much in the way of tenant improvements, capital equipment, furnishings or inventory as a restaurant does in order to operate successfully. In fact, since most of your work takes place by visiting the client's location, the consultant might not need a location at all. Yet, despite this low cost of acquisition, the consulting business might be just as profitable or even more profitable than the far more expensive restaurant.

Consulting businesses are not an isolated example of this sort of opportunity. Think about any business where someone comes to you to provide a service, rather than a business where you go to their location to receive a service. When there is a location that you go to, the business owner has had to pay to furnish and fixture it. When a particular service is done at your residence or place of business, all that the service provider needs to successfully perform the service is the equipment required to provide the service, and a way to travel to your home or office. Starting to get the picture?

Here are more examples. Two businesses that cost the same to start to furnish and "build out", may not, once opened, have equal ability to make money. The simplest way to prove this to you is to look at a business that operates multiple locations. As a frame of reference, think of any fast food chain that you are familiar with. While each location may be virtually identical, and therefore had equal start up costs, each location will not be equally busy, nor will they all make the same amount of profit. Some locations will simply outperform others! You knew that…didn't you? Haven't we all seen identical businesses that have locations that are always busy and always seem to have long lines, and others that seem never to be crowded? Some outlets fail altogether, but that doesn't mean that it cost less to start them. Both the great outlet and the weak one might have had identical start up costs. Sometimes, the weak one might actually have cost more than its more successful counterpart. If it's true about different locations for the same business, it's also true for different businesses in the same basic location. How many times have you visited a shopping center that has two businesses that look like they cost about the same amount to get started, but where one is doing a very brisk business, and the other is not? We all have. For me, there is a perfect example that I can think of.

There is a shopping center near my home that has two very similar fast food places. I always go to one, rather than the other because the one I go to always has the shorter line, and I'm usually in a hurry. Shorter lines are just another way of saying that it does less business than the other restaurant. Now that I've hopefully got you convinced, you're probably saying to yourself that since it isn't automatically true that the more you spend the more you will get, you should probably buy the least expensive business you can find. After all, if what I'm saying is true, and it is, doesn't that mean that everyone should buy a less expensive business, since it might do just as well or better as a more expensive alternative? Absolutely not! Surprise! I'm not saying that at all. Sometimes the more expensive business does do better than the less expensive one, and would be a much better buy for you. The point is that the correlation between investment size and investment quality is not reliable. Now you're really confused! I just spent a whole lot of time convincing you that you can get a business that can be just as good, but that costs less than another one. So, why would you ever spend more rather than less? The answer is relatively simple. Different businesses require their owners to have different skills to successfully operate them, and some more expensive businesses ARE better than others that are less expensive.

Let's go back to my earlier example of the restaurant and the consulting business. Just as it doesn't mean that the more expensive restaurant will automatically be better than the less expensive consulting business, neither does it mean that the consulting business will be successful and the restaurant a failure. Still confused? It's okay. Let's sort it out. The point that I have been trying to make is that size of investment will not, by itself, define the quality of the business that you acquire.

Steel yourself to this fact: A good business may have either a high cost of acquisition, or a low cost of acquisition, or anything in between. There will simply be no automatic correlation between the size of your investment and the quality of your opportunity. Additionally, we already know that different people like and are good at different things. It doesn't matter whether it's which movie to see, which candidate to vote for, what team to root for, or which job a person will most like and best succeed with. People are different, and these differences will have a lot to do with the type of business that is best suited to a particular buyer. The right business to buy is the one that best matches up with that buyer's skill sets, values, and goals, irrespective of that business' cost of acquisition. So what's the bottom line for you? You should not automatically spend a lot, assuming that the more you spend the more you will get. Neither, however, should you buy the least expensive business you can find, assuming that all businesses are the same. You should spend as much or as little as it takes to get the right business for you. That business not only has to have the proven ability to produce the kind of income, life, and lifestyle that you want, but also should be one where the successful owners have the same basic skills, abilities, etc. that you have. If you find a business like that, and it costs less, buy it! If it costs more, then spend the money.

Success is the goal. Just be careful not to get distracted by those pesky myths!

Keep track of the concerns that are keeping you awake at night.

End Of Chapter Notes

Use this page to write down notes, ideas and other brainstorming for buying your franchise.

Section Seven

Final steps

"We all have dreams. But in order to make dreams come into reality, it takes an awful lot of determination, dedication, self-discipline, and effort."

Jesse Owens.

Introduction

If you have come to this stage in the buying process, hopefully you have narrowed down your options to a franchise that meets your most important criteria. You will have been working with the franchisor and their team, your franchise consultant, any experts you've chosen to engage and possibly your immediate family and friends. You've read and re-read the FDD, created a multitude of business plans, checked, double-checked and triple-checked your finances, spoken extensively to the current franchisees in the system, attend the franchisor's Discovery Day and have removed all the roadblocks and nerves as best you can.

So your last major decision is to either get things going with this franchisor or move on.

If the decision is to get things going, then in simple terms the process would include:
1. Advising the franchisor so they can prepare the necessary paperwork for you to sign including the Franchise Agreement.
2. Obtain finance (if this is necessary.)
3. Confirm a date to attend Corporate training.
4. Put in motion the specifics of that franchise.

Secure Finance

Securing a loan can be a slow and frustrating process so if finance is needed by the buyer this process should have been identified and begun some time ago. The process will vary depending on the type of loan required such as an SBA loan, conventional loan, or maybe you are using a short term home equity loan. Regardless, before signing any final paperwork, check the status of your loan as it will give you road map for making "go forward" decisions.

Write down questions about the financing process so you can check later.

Obtain Lender Instructions

As we just mentioned, when third party finance is involved, the lender will require a lot of documents. While most of these are provided by the buyer, the seller is also required to provide some documentation. As the process continues, the lender may request even more documents and more information. As the owner of the business, be patient with the process and supply all documents as quickly and readily as you can so the process keeps moving.

Just so you know, if a third party lender provides financing, the time to process all the paperwork and get approval can take anywhere from 30 to 60 days, with 45 days being about the norm. If the third party lender is from the Small Business Administration, there are strict processes for the lender to follow with no shortcuts allowed. Bottom line: Respond as quickly and professionally as you can, otherwise you may end up killing the transaction.

Track requests you receive by your lender for documents:

Lender Request	Date you provided

Sign The Franchise Agreement

When you received a copy of the Franchise Disclosure Document it would have included a copy of the Franchise Agreement. This is the legal and binding agreement between you and the franchisor or, if you are working with a Master Franchise, between you and the Master Franchise. Only sign this document when you are ready. Only sign this document when you have every question answered. Only sign this document after you've spoken with an attorney and are comfortable this is the direction you wish to go. Only sign this document when you have all the finance necessary to close the transaction.

If the answer to all the items above was "I'm ready" then, congratulations! Don't underestimate those final nerves. Good luck as you move forward with your business ownership and I hope you found this guide helpful with that process.

Sign other final documents

There will be other documents to sign as you gear up your franchise and set things in motion. Your franchisor will provide you a list if it hasn't been provided already. At the end of this section I've put together a final checklist of documents to sign. It's not complete as each franchise is different but it gives you a starting point with room to add items specific to your franchise.

Create Your Legal Entity

An important item you now need to attend to, and you may have done this prior to signing the franchise agreement, is the legal entity of your company or corporation. This is a discussion item to initially have with your accountant to get their advice on the best entity for your tax situation and then complete with your attorney who can create the legal entity for you. One of your options is to do nothing and operate as a Sole Proprietor but your accountant and attorney will give you good reasons why this is probably not your best option.

Attend Corporate Training

Many things will now have been set in motion with you signing the franchise agreement and require fairly quick action. One of the main items will be attending corporate training provided by the franchise. Each franchise conducts the training on a schedule that works for them and they will usually advise you well in advance. The purpose of this training is to provide a strategic overview of the business, how it operates, the Home Office culture and your contact points.

As a suggestion, when attending corporate training, because it may only be a monthly occurrence, make sure you plan and be ready to attend the training. So much information will be provided by your franchisor so make sure you are rested and ready to absorb as much knowledge as you can in short period of time.

Attend Local Training

Once again, this is not necessarily typical of all franchises, but some include corporate training while others include local training especially if the franchise includes a Master franchise. The critical piece is to make sure that you are rested and ready to learn the tactical operations as either your business is now open or will be once you complete this training.

Write down any questions you have about any of the above processes to check with your consultant, advisor or franchisor:

Final Checklist

On the following page is the beginning of a checklist. The checklist is not exhaustive but gives a good starting point with room for you to add other items as they relate to the franchise you've just bought.

And by the way, congratulations! If you are reading this part of the guide because your journey has come to this point, then your business is now yours and I wish you nothing but success.

Well done!

Description	Start Date	Completion Date	Contact
Franchise application submitted			
Attend Franchisor Discovery Day for approval			
Due diligence/validations completed			
All purchase documents signed			
Lender finance applications signed and submitted			
Corporation filing, Fed ID# and fictitious name filing with County Office			
Open bank account(s) with checks and deposit slips (bank will need Fed ID# and copy of legal entity if a LLC, Partnership or Corporation)			
Insurance: Worker's Compensation; Business; Vehicles; Life			
Lease of premises applied for (if applicable.)			
Determine bookkeeping method: QuickBooks? Print checks/write checks?			
Set up payroll payment process with a vendor			
Credit card processing application & set up (if applicable.)			
Finalize any equipment leases (and delivery)			
Determine processes to handle cash drawer: money, daily receipts and deposits			

Description	Start Date	Completion Date	Contact
Determine how to transfer business records: hard and soft copies			
Organize utilities: Electricity; telephone; long distance; water; trash/sewer Fire Dept./Health Dept. inspection (if applicable)			
Contact vendors to establish credit and relationship			
Ensure all employees have completed HR requirements such as I-9, W-2's etc.			
Organize business contact phone numbers			
Vehicle title; equipment leases			
Document all employee contacts in case of emergency			
Hire employees (if applicable)			
Set up and document emergency business procedures for employees to follow			
Ensure adequate inventory available (if applicable)			
Apply for Business license with your local City Office			
Apply for Re-sale permit (sales tax permit) with State Board of Equalization (If applicable.)			
Apply for State Employer ID # (SEIN) with Employee Development Department (EDD)			
Apply and obtain any additional Licenses required for your industry/business.			

End Of Chapter Notes

Use this page to write down final notes, ideas and other brainstorming for buying your franchise.

Additional Information

"*Working hard overcomes a whole lot of other obstacles. You can have unbelievable intelligence, you can have connections, you can have opportunities fall out of the sky. But in the end, hard work is the true, enduring characteristic of successful people.* "

Rear Admiral Marsha Evans

Introduction

The following introduces a few different options that may be of interest to a franchise buyer when looking for sources of third party finance. Third party finance options are many and varied but here a few highlights.

SBA Programs

The Small Business Administration (SBA) has a range of loan programs available for qualifying businesses. There are two types of lenders: a Non-Preferred Lender and a Preferred Lender. Finding a Preferred Lender is generally the best option as these lenders are empowered to make credit decisions for the SBA. Preferred Lenders include banks, national lenders such as CIT, and popular small business and regional lenders such as Comerica and PNC.

There are extensive rules and regulations to follow that cover the SBA loan program and the lenders are also subject to conflicts of interest and ethical requirements. For example, it is very difficult for a buyer to borrow funds if they have a federal felony conviction. It is also highly unlikely to obtain a loan approval if it is to buy "a house of ill-repute," as it was called in the old days. Sex may sell but it doesn't mean you can get an SBA loan to borrow money to buy a business that engages in it.

To purchase a small business, the loan is usually either a 7(a) or 504 loan. A 7(a) loan is available to purchase a business between $25,000 and $2,000,000. However, a lot of lenders are not interested in loans under $100,000 due to the high cost of processing and meeting compliance requirements. If real estate is involved, a 504 loan would be used and the deal can go up to $6,000,000 in total finance.

For a buyer to be eligible for an SBA loan they must:
- ✓ Intend to run the business (it must be owner operated, not an investment),
- ✓ Be a US citizen (resident aliens may apply but INS gets involved, taking more time),
- ✓ Be at least 21 years old, and
- ✓ The business must have cash flow to meet the debt service.

For more information on the SBA programs, visit: http://www.sba.gov or send me an email at info@andrew-rogerson.com so I can connect you with a lender.

Other Finance Options

Franchisor

Some franchisors will provide finance to a suitably qualified franchisee. Don't forget to ask about this option or look in the FDD as it should be mentioned there.

BORSA

BORSA stands for Business Owners Retirement Savings Account. This is a tool which allows you to fund the purchase of a franchise, business start-up or business property using your holdings in your 401(a) pension, profit sharing 401(k), 403(b), 457, IRA rollover or Roth IRA. Through the utilization of a BORSA, these purchases can be accomplished without distributions, taxes, penalties or the use of loans.

A leading provider of BORSA programs is DRDA. You can get more information from their website at http://www.drdacpa.com.

Guidant Financial Group

If you are looking for funds to purchase your franchise, one option may be to use the existing funds in your IRA. Guidant Financial Group is able to advise a buyer on how to use a self-directed structure to access their retirement funds.

For more information, visit the Guidant website at http://www.guidantfinancial.com.

SD Cooper

Your 401K or IRA account may be used to fund the purchase of a business including starting a new franchise. SD Cooper provides a service that allows a buyer to put the right structure in place. For more information, visit their website at http://www.sdcooper.com.

> *"Apply yourself. Get all the education you can get, but then, by God, do something. Don't just stand there, make it happen."*
>
> *Lee Iacocca*

Additional Sources Of Information

Attorney

American Bar Association   http://www.abanet.org/forums/franchising

Books

Small Business Books   http://www.smallbizbooks.com
Amazon   http://www.amazon.com
Borders   http://www.borders.com
Books Online   http://www.booksonline.com

Coaching/Knowledge

Business.com   http://www.business.com
Franklin Covey   https://www.franklincoveycoaching.com
The Alternative Board   http://www.tabboards.com
Society of Competitive Intelligence Professionals   http://www.scip.org

Franchise Association

International Franchise Association   http://www.franchise.org
Information on publicly traded franchises   http://www.freeedgar.com

General Business Websites

Small Business Administration   http://sba.gov
IRS   http://www.irs.gov
Yahoo Finance   http://finance.yahoo.com
MSN Money   http://moneycentral.msn.com/home.asp
Stat-USA   http://www.stat-usa.gov
The Deal   http://www.thedeal.com
The Wall Street Journal   http://online.wsj.com/small-business

Magazines

Inc. Magazine   http://www.inc.com
Success Magazine   http://www.success
Entrepreneur Magazine   http://www.entrepreneur.com
Forbes Magazine   http://www.forbes.com
Business Week   http://www.businessweek.com

Publicly traded franchises

More information on publicly traded franchises   http://www.freeedgar.com

Other Resources

Small Business Development Center (SBDC)

The Small Business Development Centers provide management assistance to small businesses. To find your local SBDC office, check here: http://sbdcnet.org/sbdc.php

SCORE - Service Corp Of Retired Executives (SCORE)

This national organization has local chapters full of experienced business professionals that have "been there, done that" and wish to give back to their local business community by providing a free consultation/mentoring service.
For more information about SCORE: http://www.score.org
To find a local chapter near you: http://www.score.org/explore_score.html

Chambers of Commerce

http://www.uschamber.com

The Learning Annex

http://www.learningannex.com

End Of Chapter Notes

Use this page to write down notes, ideas and other brainstorming for buying your franchise.

Glossary

The following glossary references some of the terms you may come across as you buy your franchise.

- **Account:** In the bookkeeping sense, account means a basic category of information in which the financial effects of transactions are recorded. For example, consider a checkbook. It provides an account or itemization of the cash inflows and outflows of the balance of your checking account such as health expense, rent expense, entertainment expense, cash, etc.

- **Accounting Method:** A process under which income and expenses are determined for tax purposes. This includes both the cash and accrual procedures.

- **Accounting Period:** The 12-month period that a taxpayer uses to determine federal income tax liability.

- **Accounts Payable (AP):** Amount of money owed to suppliers by the owner of the business that are not paid for by cash but on terms of credit agreed to by both parties.

- **Accounts Receivable (AR):** Amount of money owed by customers to the owner of the business that is not paid for by cash but on terms of credit agreed to by both parties.

- **Accrual Method of Accounting:** One of the two most common methods of accounting. Under this method, income is reported in the tax year earned, whether or not received, and deductions are claimed in the tax year incurred, whether or not paid.

- **Accrued Interest:** Interest that has been earned but not yet paid or credited.

- **Acknowledgement of Receipt definition:** The last page of an Offering Circular which indicates the receipt of the documents on a certain date. This, when signed and returned, acts as proof of the date one received the documents.

- **Advertising Fee:** Annual fee that is paid by the franchisee to the franchisor as his share of the corporate advertising expenditures. This advertising fee is charged by few franchisors only.

- **Agent:** Appointed individual who can act on behalf of the person or entity. The corporation is legally bound by the actions of the agent.

- **Amortization:** Similar to depreciation but applies to intangible assets such as leasehold improvements.

- **Approved Products:** Those products which a franchisee must buy from the franchisor. It also includes products which must be bought from approved suppliers. This is done by the franchisor in order to maintain quality across all franchisees.

- **Arbitration:** A way of resolving disputes by referring them to a third party which is selected by the parties.

- **Area Development Rights:** The rights allocated to a franchisee to operate a number of franchises within a specific geographic area.

- **Area Franchise:** A franchisee licensed to develop a particular area. This Area Franchisee sometimes includes performance targets and schedules. It can also include franchise sales rights.

- **Assignment Fees:** The monthly fees paid by the franchisee to the franchise company for expenses incurred by the company like corporate marketing and advertising.

- **Asset:** Anything owned that has economic value such as a truck, cash, inventory, etc.

- ➤ **Assumed Name:** *see DBA*

- ➤ **Balance Sheet (BS):** A statement of the financial status of the business on a certain date ("snapshot").

- ➤ **Basis:** The amount assigned to an asset from which gain or loss is determined for income tax purposes when the asset is sold. For assets acquired by purchase, this is the cost including other allowed adjustments such as depreciation.

- ➤ **Blue Sky:** That portion of a "claimed" value or requested price that cannot be supported or generally shown to exist through the application of established valuation methodology. Blue sky is different from Goodwill.

- ➤ **Book Value:** The depreciated value of an asset found on the balance sheet. This can be calculated by subtracting accumulated depreciation from the cost of the related asset.

- ➤ **Broker:** An intermediary between the buyer and the seller. He can represent either the buyer or the seller, and in some cases even both parties.

- ➤ **Business Format Franchise:** In Business Format Franchise the franchisor gives the permission to the franchisee for use of product, service and trademark. The entire business format is also taught to the franchisee including marketing, selling, inventory, accounting and personnel procedures.

- ➤ **Capital Required:** The amount of cash one is required to have available.

- ➤ **Cash Basis Accounting:** A method of accounting wherein income and expenses are recognized, within the statements, when the business receives the income or pays the expense. *Also see Accrual Basis Accounting.*

- ➤ **Cash Flow:** Basically, the business' net income plus non-cash charges (depreciation, amortization, and depletion). It can be defined as before or after such items as taxes, debt service (interest only or principal and interest) or extraordinary items. (Should not be confused with Net Cash Flow, a.k.a. Free Cash Flow.)

- ➤ **Cash Method of Accounting:** One of the two most common methods of accounting with the other being Accrual. Under this method of accounting, income is reported in the tax year received and expenses are deducted in the tax year paid. *see Accrual Basis Accounting.*

- ➤ **Chart of Accounts:** The formal index of all the accounts used by the business to record its transactions.

- ➤ **Conversion Franchise:** A franchise system permitting existing businesses to join a national franchise system and be able to use its name, trademark and operating system.

- ➤ **Copyright:** Form of protection under the law for authors to protect "original works of authorship." This protection is available for both published and unpublished works.

- ➤ **Corporation:** A legal business entity owned by shareholders with the ability to own property, incur debts and sue or be sued. For income tax purposes, this term includes associations, trusts that have a majority of corporate characteristics, joint stock companies and insurance companies.

- ➤ **Cost of Goods Sold/Cost of Sales** (CGS, COGS, COS): A grouping of expenses applicable to the materials and labor incorporated directly in the goods or services delivered and sold.

- ➤ **DBA (Doing Business As):** An assumed name under which a business conducts business. For example, Billy Bob Enterprises, Inc. DBA Billy Bob's Hot Dog Grill and Bar.

- ➤ **Default:** The failure to perform as was agreed upon by the parties.

- ➤ **Depreciation:** The deduction of a reasonable allowance for the wear and tear of assets (excluding inventory) used in a trade or business or held for the production of income.

➢ **Disclosure:** Refers to revealing facts to others. In a franchise these facts may be complimentary to the franchisor, such as disclosing a prior bankruptcy or litigation.

➢ **Discretionary Earnings:** Adjusted earnings before taxes, interest income or expense, non-operating and non-recurring expenses, depreciation and other non-cash charges and prior to deducting an owners/officers compensation.

➢ **Distributorship:** The right granted by a manufacturer or a wholesaler for distribution or sale of products. Distributorship does not generally qualify as a franchisee. However, certain franchisees can qualify as a distributorship.

➢ **Domestic Corporation:** A corporation in the state where it has been incorporated.

➢ **Earnings Claims:** Assertions made by franchise companies of specific acquired sales levels or profitability levels.

➢ **EIN (Employer Identification Number):** *See Federal Tax Identification Number.*

➢ **Employee:** An individual that provides services to a business and is distinguished differently from an independent contractor. This is important because the withholding of incomes taxes on wage applies only to this individual.

➢ **Entrepreneur:** The Person who assumes the responsibility for organizing and operating the business. He also assumes the risk including the financial risk for a business venture.

➢ **Equity:** The recorded "value" of the ownership interest in a business entity. Also known as Owner's Equity.

➢ **Estimated (Useful) Life:** Period of time over which an asset will be used by a particular taxpayer.

➢ **Exclusive Territory:** Gives the right of the territory to the franchisee preventing the franchisor from appointing any other franchisee for the territory or carrying on business himself in the territory.

➢ **Expense:** An item charged against revenue in the income statement for something that is used up during the income statement period of time.

➢ **Fair Market Value (FMV):** The amount at which property would change hands between a willing buyer and a willing seller, neither being under compulsion to buy or sell and both having reasonable knowledge of the relevant facts.

➢ **Federal Tax Identification Number:** This is a number assigned to a corporation or other business entity by the federal government for tax purposes. This is also known as EIN (Employer Identification Number).

➢ **FICA (Federal Insurance Contributions Act):** The law that provides for Social Security and Medicare benefits. This program is financed by payroll taxes imposed equally on the employer and the employee. A person self-employed will pay both the employer and employee portion of this tax which is known as self-employment tax.

➢ **Fiscal Year:** Any period of exactly or approximately 12 months used by a business as its accounting period. Some retail businesses always close their yearend on a Saturday and therefore will have either 52 or 53 weeks in a fiscal year.

➢ **Foreign Corporation:** A corporation not organized under the laws of one of the states or territories of the United States. This description relates to the federal level as this term is also used by each state to describe a corporation doing business in the state but organized under another states laws.

- **Franchise:** Permission given by a person or entity permitting the distribution of goods or services under his trademark, service mark or trade name by an agreement to another person or entity. During this period the grantor retains control over the franchisee.

- **Franchise Business Plan:** A strategic plan that lays down the company's objectives and the specific steps that need to be taken to achieve those objectives. The Business Plan is usually prepared by company management.

- **Franchise Fee:** Fee initially paid by the franchisee to the franchisor to acquire the franchise.

- **Goodwill:** The ability of a business to generate income in excess of a normal rate on assets due to superior managerial skills, market position, new product technology, etc.

- **Gross Profit:** That portion of Net Sales that remains after the subtraction of the Cost of Goods Sold. This is sometimes called Gross Margin.

- **Housemark:** A trademark which is used to identify the operations of an organization. This may in certain cases also be the company name. This trademark is used to identify one or more products and at times is used in combination with other trademarks.

- **Income:** All sources of business income; may be synonymous with Revenue or Sales.

- **Income Statement (IS):** A financial statement used to report the financial results of a business' operations during the period of time specified within the statement. Also known as the Profit and Loss or P&L.

- **Independent Contractor:** Taxpayer who contracts to do work according to his own methods and who is not subject to control except as to the results of such work. An employee, by contrast, is subject to the control of the employer as to the methods to be used to obtain the desired results.

- **Industry:** The category of business to which a franchise belongs. It is an all-encompassing area of business that can incorporate several different sectors.

- **Intangible Personal Property:** Assets, other than real property, with no intrinsic value; their value lies in the rights conveyed. Examples include cash, insurance, stock, goodwill, and patents.

- **International Franchise Association (IFA):** Based in Washington, D.C., a trade association for franchisors.

- **Inventory:** List of articles of property. For income tax purposes, this refers only to a list of articles comprising stock in trade–articles held for sale to customers in the regular course of a trade or business.

- **Lessee:** One who rents property from another. In the case of real estate, the lessee is also known as the tenant.

- **Lessor:** One who rents property to another. In the case of real estate, the lessor is also known as the landlord.

- **Limited Liability Company (LLC):** Operating structure contains the liability protection of a corporation and the flexibility of a partnership.

- **Liquidation:** The process of converting securities or other property into cash.

- **Marketing Plan:** Detailed plan setting the marketing activities of the organization.

- **Master Franchise:** Individual or a company which owns the exclusive rights to develop a particular geographic area.

- **NAICS (North American Industry Classification System) Code:** A system of numbering that assigns a unique number to each business industry and thereby allows for collection and comparison of statistical information within an industry. *Also see SIC code.*

➤ **Operations Manual:** Covers all the aspects of the business and consists of guidelines for the franchisee on how to operate the franchised business.

➤ **Ownership:** A generic term meaning 100% controlling ownership.

➤ **Partnership:** Form of business in which two or more persons join their money and skills in conducting the business. This form is treated as a conduit and is not subject to taxation.

➤ **Patent:** Legal protection for an inventor. If issued, a patent grants "the right to exclude others from making, using, offering for sale, or selling" the invention. There are three types of patents: design, utility and plant.

➤ **Perquisites (Perks):** Special additional benefits received as compensation because of position. In privately held businesses these are often a result of the ability of the business to pay for them, more than a result of market rate compensation for the services provided to the business. For example, company-paid vehicles, insurance, travel, memberships, etc.

➤ **Prepaid Expense:** The capitalized payment for items such as rent, insurance, etc. that cover more than one year. Cash-basis as well as accrual-basis taxpayers usually are required to capitalize these types of costs.

➤ **Product Format Franchise:** Where the franchised product or service does not constitute the majority of the products or services on offer by the franchisee.

➤ **Pro forma statements:** Statements issued by the franchisor to the franchisee based on actual operating results of the franchisor's units or franchise establishments. It can be in the form of any statement which measures profits and expenses.

➤ **Protected Territory:** Territory allotted to a franchisee where the franchisor has promised not to franchise to another franchisee or open a company owned business.

➤ **Public Figure Involvement:** When a public figure is endorsing a franchised product then the nature of the agreement between the public figure and the franchisor must be disclosed.

➤ **Qualification Questionnaire:** Document prepared by the franchisor to seek information from a prospective franchise.

➤ **Quality Control:** The method used by the franchisor to enforce the rules set in the operating manuals. Quality control involves regional coordinators visiting each franchisee.

➤ **Royalty:** The franchisee is required to pay to the franchisor a percentage of the gross sales on a monthly basis.

➤ **S Corporation:** An elective provision permitting certain small business corporations and their shareholders to elect special income tax treatment. Of major significance is the fact that this election usually avoids the corporate income tax and corporate losses can be claimed by the shareholders.

➤ **Section 179 Expense Deduction:** An election to treat the cost of certain qualified property as a currently deductible expense rather than as a capital expenditure. This treatment is also referred to as expensing. A maximum deduction, adjusted annually, may be claimed for qualified assets placed in service during the year. This deduction may be further limited based on the total cost of depreciable assets placed in service during the year.

➤ **Sector:** The categories included within a broader scope of franchise opportunities. It is also known as the Industry.

- ➢ **SIC (Standard Industrial Classification) Code or NAICS (North American Industry Classification System) Code:** System of numbering that assigns a unique number to each business industry. This allows for collection and comparison of statistical information within an industry.

- ➢ **Slick:** Pre-paid piece of advertising material which the franchisor gives to the franchisee for use in local print media.

- ➢ **Source Documents:** Virtually every business transaction needs documentation which is known as a source document or supporting documentation (back-up). Examples include check register, invoice, receipt, purchase order, etc.

- ➢ **Start Up Costs:** The investment required to be made by the franchisee at the start of the franchise.

- ➢ **Total Investment:** Initial investment, the working capital, and subsequent additions to inventory and equipment which will be necessary for the fully operational and profitable enterprise.

- ➢ **Trade Secret:** Are revealed to the franchisee by the franchise transaction.

- ➢ **Trademark:** Word, name, symbol, or device that is used in trade with goods to indicate the source of the goods and to distinguish them from the goods of others.

- ➢ **Turnkey:** The franchisor is expected to provide the platform to run the business to the franchisee, even without any input from the franchisee.

- ➢ **Working Capital:** Excess of the value of the current assets over the value of the current liabilities.

Other Books In This Series

If you've always thought you would like to own and operate your own business but were never sure where to start, this is the guide for you. This 174 page workbook starts by asking the question if business ownership is for you. It then explains the options available to you and then takes you through, in detail, a step by step process to determining what sort of business you can buy, what you will need to buy a business, and, how to evaluate a business for sale. It also includes the steps to prepare for business ownership with your legal entity, understanding business licenses and permits, how to obtain finance to buy a business, accounting processes and terms, financial planning tools such as profit and loss projectors, sales forecasts, how to create business plans, sales and marketing plans. There are lots of checklists, resources, other planning sheets and tools so when you buy your business you are up and running as quickly as possible for maximum profit.

Are you considering business ownership and not sure where to start? If so, you have three options. Buy an existing business, buy the rights to a franchise or start your own business from scratch. This 182 page workbook includes how to decide which industry is right for you, how to create your legal entity, obtain business permits and licenses and business insurance. It also explains how to build your dream business using the solid foundations of a business plan, sales and marketing plan and productivity plan, all dovetailed with financial planning tools such as startup costs planners, profit and loss projectors, sales forecasts, break even analyses and more. It also includes finance options, checklists, resources, other planning sheets and tools to start your business as quickly as possible. Finally, this workbook shows how to do all this and more with the focus that a buyer may wish to buy your business and if so, what processes you would follow to sell for the highest price.

Thinking about selling your business? This 150 page comprehensive workbook helps you understand the many complexities and decisions you have to make. Written by a professional business broker with many years of real world business experience, this guide shows you how to sell your business in the shortest possible time for the best possible price. It includes reasons why you need to plan ahead for taxes, how to avoid potential legal, accounting, and other roadblocks, how to value your business and other assets, the different types of professionals available and how to research and properly prepare for selling. Also includes how to search for and qualify potential buyers, address finance concerns, protect you and your business with confidentiality agreements, prepare an executive summary, confidential business review and conduct effective negotiations. Also includes dozens of worksheets, checklists, and charts for you to track during the steps of selling.

About The Author

Andrew Rogerson currently holds the Certified Business Intermediary (CBI) designation from the International Business Brokers Association (IBBA), the highest designation awarded by the IBBA. Andrew has also earned the Certified Business Broker (CBB) designation from the California Association of Business Brokers. He holds a Certified Machinery and Equipment designation (CMEA) from the National Business and Builders Institute and is a Certified Senior Business Analyst (CSBA) with the Society of Business Analysts. He also holds a Brokers License with the California Department of Real Estate.

As the owner and managing director of Rogerson Business Services in Sacramento, CA, Andrew assists his clients with both selling and buying businesses.

Since 1983, Andrew has owned and operated five businesses. At just 27 years old, he bought his first business, an international travel agency. With hard work resulting in increased sales, Andrew sold the travel agency just two years later for 2 1/2 times his original purchase price.

Andrew's next venture involved owning and managing two retail office equipment/furniture stores, followed by a wholesale travel and tourism company based in Los Angeles that had an annual turnover of $10,000,000. More recently, Andrew and his wife Anne owned an executive suites business in Fair Oaks, CA. Anne operated this business while Andrew worked as an outsourced program manager at the Roseville campus of Hewlett Packard. At HP, Andrew managed a team of 42 employees, deploying a new global call center and support team that included Web developers, technical writers and trainers.

Andrew was educated at La Trobe University in Melbourne, Australia, his native country, and recently completed studies in Business Valuation and Appraisals and Business Brokerage. Andrew and Anne have two daughters, Belinda and Catherine and reside in Sacramento, California. Andrew enjoys flying (he is pursuing his pilot's license) and SCUBA diving as well as sports and politics.

Contact Andrew for Assistance with Buying or Selling a Business

Andrew offers a broad range of services including business valuations, transaction analysis, consulting for business sellers and buyers, consulting for buyers considering franchise ownership and appraisals for machinery and equipment.

The combination of Andrew's hands-on experience in the business buying and selling process, his diverse background in a variety of industries and his international business experience makes him an ideal choice for a business intermediary.

Call Andrew Rogerson at (916) 570-2674 or send him an e-mail at info@Andrew-Rogerson.com to discuss how you can put his knowledge and experience to work for you.

Visit Andrew's website: www.Andrew-Rogerson.com

www.ingramcontent.com/pod-product-compliance
Lightning Source LLC
Chambersburg PA
CBHW081454170526
45166CB00008B/2428